Creating my own Nemesis

by John Wardley

The autobiography of the man
who designed Alton Towers'
big rides, and brought the
Theme Park to Britain

First published in Great Britain 2013

Seventh edition 2017

Copyright ©John Wardley 2017

www.john-wardley.co.uk

All rights reserved. No part of this publication may be reproduced or transmitted in any form or by any means, electronic or mechanical including photocopying, recording or any information storage or retrieval system, without prior permission from the Author.

**This book is dedicated to the memory of
Jack Jay
who gave me my first insight into the world of
Showbusiness**

I gratefully acknowledge the help I have been given in
writing this book by
Scott Scott, Mike Peake, Stephen Jenkins, Hugh Allison
and my wife Jenny

Chapter 1

THE SEEDS ARE SOWN

The headline in the Rochdale Observer for Tuesday 20th. February 1923 read:

"Famous Russian illusionist predicts Saturday's local football score"

And underneath:

"Last night on stage at the Rochdale Hippodrome, the famous Russian illusionist Vadir, accompanied by his lovely assistant Dorinova, predicted the score of this Saturday's football match between Rochdale A.F.C and Bolton Wanderers. Vadir secretly wrote his prediction on a piece of paper which was locked inside a small wooden box. This was given to Mr. Mossop, Manager of the Co-operative Bank in Yorkshire Street, with the strict instructions that he should lock it in his safe and that it should remain in his possession until next Saturday evening, when he should return to the stage of the Hippodrome and open the box to reveal if the prediction is true."

34 years later, as a seven year old boy, I sat at the feet of my great uncle Tommy in his little cottage just outside the village of Hoxne in Suffolk, reading the brown and crumbling newspaper clipping. "Were you right, uncle?" I asked. "Of course I was" he replied. "I was always right."

Although crippled with arthritis, Great Uncle Tommy was a bright 72 year old. In the first three decades of the 20th. century, Vadir and Dorinova were a music hall variety act that toured theatres all over Britain. They were neither "famous" nor "Russian" (the closest they ever got to Russia was Felixstowe, and that was by accident, having got on the wrong train connection at Ipswich), but they made a decent living.

Tommy McKay was born in North Shields in 1885, and was my mother's uncle. "Dorinova" was in fact his wife, my great aunt Rene. They had started out as an acrobatic novelty act "Vadir and Dorinova – and the Dive of Death". This consisted of Tommy throwing Rene around the stage in various acrobatic manoeuvres, accompanied by suitably dramatic music, before the grand finale when she would climb a ladder up into one of the auditorium boxes and jump from the parapet of the box onto Tommy's shoulders onstage whilst performing a somersault in mid-flight. The act was suddenly terminated after an unfortunate incident in Wolverhampton when she missed her target and plummeted into the orchestra pit. Fortunately she was saved by a fortuitously-placed kettle drum which acted like a trampoline and broke her fall. The "Dive of Death" was never to be attempted again.

Not letting this setback end their career, a new act was conceived. Tommy had served his apprenticeship as a cabinet-maker in the late 1800s. He had watched the acts of various illusionists who performed on the same bill as them, and he decided to use his carpentry skills to build an illusion act. This consisted mainly of putting "Dorinova" in one of numerous boxes that filled the stage, and doing diabolical things to them ... sawing them in half, sticking swords through them, winching them up on pulleys and letting them crash to the stage floor and so on. All very spectacular, but nothing the audiences hadn't seen before. Something different was needed.

By chance, while performing in York he ran into an old school friend of his who had been apprenticed as a locksmith. After a few pints in a nearby pub, the idea of Tommy becoming an escapologist was drunkenly discussed ... and eventually dismissed (there were far too many escapologists playing the halls at that time). But the pair then came up with another idea which was to turn around the fortunes of Vadir and Dorinova, and combine Tommy's cabinet-making skills with the craft of his locksmith friend. The Prediction Chest was created.

Weekly variety in the early years of the 20th. century was just that ... a new show every week. Monday to Saturday the acts performed, and then on Sunday moved on to the next town for the next week's show. What theatre managers desperately looked for were acts that could hit the headlines in the papers early in the week to pull the audiences in for the remaining performances of that week's show. As the cutting from the Rochdale Observer shows, uncle's Prediction Chest act did just that.

I watched as Uncle Tommy creakily rose from his comfy armchair by the fire, and went into the kitchen. The fire in their cottage burned day and night, winter and summer, through blizzards and heatwaves. The smells of applewood burning on the fire, and spicy fruitcakes baking in the oven remind me of their tiny cluttered cottage to this day.

The sound of a stuck cupboard door being wrenched open in the kitchen, followed by the clatter of a landslide of its contents tumbling onto the kitchen floor could be heard, and then Auntie Rene's voice "Tom, what are you looking for?". "I want to show the boy THE BOX" came the reply. I sat in stunned anticipation. I was actually going to see THE BOX.

Eventually the old man returned clutching a polished wooden chest, slightly larger than a shoe box, with a large brass lock and keyhole. It was not locked, and on opening the hinged lid I saw it contained a collection of old posters and photographs of their performing years. Tommy's arthritic hands had difficulty extracting these, but once they were removed I could see in the bottom was a beautifully ornate brass key. "Rene, bring me a scrap of paper and a pencil" Tommy shouted into the kitchen. Dutifully, my aunt returned with the desired articles. "I am going to write on this piece of paper the headline that is going to appear on the front page of tomorrow morning's Daily Mail", he dramatically announced. He scribbled something on the paper, rolled it up tightly, and dropped it into the box. Then he inserted the key in the lock and turned it, the action producing a most satisfyingly precision-engineered "clunk" as the mechanism operated to lock the box. "Now, John, you are not to let this casket out of your sight until midday tomorrow, when you can open it and read what that piece of paper says".

I took the box from him, and put it on my lap. For the next 24 hours the box went everywhere with me. That night it was safely hidden under the bed-clothes next to me. It went with me to the bathroom, and at breakfast the next day I put it on the breakfast table next to the cornflakes and made sure Uncle Tommy never touched it. At around 10 o'clock there was a flopping sound on the mat by the front door as the paper boy delivered the day's newspaper.

The big moment had arrived. We opened the paper and the headline on the Daily Mail's front page read:

"Hydrogen bomb detonated on Christmas Island"

This was the second of a series of nine nuclear explosions that the British used to covertly test their prototype hydrogen bombs under the codename "Operation Grapple".

Uncle Tommy handed me the key to the box. This mysterious casket had been in my possession since the previous day. The bomb had exploded during the night under the greatest of secrecy. There was no way he could have known about this in advance. Gingerly I inserted the key in the lock and turned it. I opened the lid. Inside was the rolled-up piece of paper. I unrolled it. Written in a shaky hand were the words:

"Hydrogen bomb detonated on Christmas Island"

It was to be three more years before I discovered the secret of the Prediction Chest. And I am going to share that secret with you. But first, I had to prove my worth.

Vadir & Dorinova perform "The Dive of Death"

The British hydrogen bomb test explosion

on Christmas Island 1957

I have always had a very ambivalent attitude towards magicians. They tend to fall into three types:

    1)   The Show-off. These people invariably have poor self-esteem and can only fit-in socially by trying to prove that they are cleverer than you. Their whole *raison d'être* is to metaphorically say to their audience "I bet you don't know how I did that. Aren't I clever!"

    2)   The Geek. These people will devote hours to perfect some obscure skill (manipulating cards, cutting and restoring pieces of rope, making coins appear from nowhere etc.). The pleasure they get is from actually honing these skills, and the demonstration of them to an audience is almost unimportant.

    3)   The Entertainer. This type of performer has only one objective ... to change the emotional state of the audience ... In other words to amaze, amuse, thrill, baffle, and give them some fun.

It is this last type that I can identify with. They aren't trying to show off, or appear superior. Their ego is not part of their motivation. They just want to give people a good time ... to take them out of the hum-drum of their everyday lives ... and if they make a fool of themselves in the process, so be it!

I have never enjoyed performing. It doesn't come naturally to me. But the wonder and amazement I experienced as a seven year-old kid in that little cottage in Suffolk made me determined that somehow I was going to be an entertainer.

But there was a big problem to overcome ..... The Family Business

The firm of Wiggins & Wardley Ltd. (established 1874) was one of the oldest printing firms in London. In the 1950s it was the only printing company located within the hallowed square mile of the City of London, with its premises in George Street, next to the Mansion House. The Wiggins side of the business was long-gone, and my father was the head of the company. And his young son John (me!) was being lined-up at a very early age to take over the family business.

Two more diverse family career backgrounds could not be imagined. On the one side was my mother's family ... the bohemian world of the Variety Artiste. On the other was my father's family business ... the establishment and the formality of trade in the City of London. But more on that later. For now, I was going to have FUN!

A visit to stay with Uncle Tommy and Auntie Rene in Suffolk was something I enjoyed every summer. Whereas other kids were given David Nixon Magic Sets for Christmas and performed little party tricks with ping-pong balls and cardboard tubes, Uncle Tommy helped me build miniature versions of the big illusions that Vadir and Dorinova used to perform 50 years previously. These would be transported back home on the roof-rack of our Austin A40 car, much to the consternation of the neighbours who knew that their kids were about to be sawn in half, set on fire, or levitated up to the ceiling. The garage would be converted into the "Palace of Illusion" and shows would be staged for the neighbourhood featuring such amazing feats as "The Sword Cabinet of Doom", "The Headless Lady" (except that at eight years of age, Sheila Watson could hardly be called a lady) and "The Metamorphosis Substitution Trunk" (I never understood what "metamorphosis" meant, but Uncle Tommy told me that's what it should be called).

I was never particularly bothered whether I performed the illusions myself, or let one of my little friends do it. I was just as happy backstage (if you could call three tables pushed together with a pair of bed-sheets as a back-cloth a "stage"). All I cared about was that the audience had a good time. I wanted them to be amazed, intrigued, mystified, thrilled. That's what mattered. And I was now nine years old.

The Prediction Chest was constantly on my mind. What was the secret? I asked Uncle Tommy what I had to do to prove myself. He lived 120 miles away from our home in Middlesex, and a visit to him that winter was out of the question. So he agreed that if I could borrow a Super-8 movie camera and film one of my illusions, then post it to him, he would judge whether I was worthy of his secret. I decided the Metamorphosis Substitution Trunk was to be the chosen illusion as it was purely visual and required no soundtrack (and, of course, Super-8 movies were silent in those days). For those that don't know the effect, a girl is put in handcuffs, inside a sack, which is put inside a box. The lid is put on the box, and ropes are bound round the box to secure the lid. The magician then jumps on top of the box, briefly holds up a curtain in front of him, drops it, and there is the girl standing on top of the box. On opening the box, who should be inside, in the bag, in the handcuffs, but … you guessed it … the magician!

Now, although I say it myself, I was pretty good at this. At nine years of age I was very agile (and so was Sheila Watson) and we could do the changeover faster than most professionals on the TV. We filmed it, posted it to Uncle Tommy, and back came the reply that next summer when I visited him he would let me into the secret of the Prediction Chest. Better than that, he promised that when he died, he'd leave the Chest to me in his will.

Winter and Spring couldn't pass quickly enough for me.

And then summer arrived.

Chapter 2

THE SECRET'S REVEALED

The car journey from Harrow to Suffolk seemed endless.

In 1960, Britain had no motorways, and what would now take just a few hours was an all-day event in that little Austin Cambridge (we had risen from the humble A40 to a Cambridge by now). Everything seemed to be conspiring against me getting to my uncle and aunt's cottage and learning the secret of the Prediction Chest. It was Royston Carnival Week, and traffic through the town was pitifully slow. "All we need now is to find the races are on in Newmarket" joked my father. It turned out to be no joke. It was Newmarket Race Week too.

Even the last couple of miles were a disaster. We always managed to get lost negotiating the narrow lanes around the village of Hoxne where their cottage nestled, and this time was no exception. But eventually we arrived. Smoke was curling out of the chimney even though it was a warm summer's day, and I could see from the apple orchard across the lane that major pruning had been taking place, so I knew the familiar smell of the smoke would greet us when the front door was opened. We knocked on the door, and waited. And waited.

A shuffling sound could be heard approaching, and eventually, after what seemed an eternity, a very hunched old figure opened it. Uncle Tommy had aged enormously since we had seen him the previous year. Although only 75, his arthritis had worsened considerably. Even he acknowledged the cause was the abuse his body had taken as a young man in the early years of "Vadir and Dorinova" (I had seen a publicity photo of them in their heyday, with Tommy balanced between two chairs in the splits, and Auntie Rene performing a handstand on his head!). Auntie eventually appeared over his shoulder, and she seemed in no better health. Something inside me told me it might not be long before I actually <u>owned</u> THE BOX.

My parents were going to drop me off to stay at the cottage for the week while they carried on to Hull to stay with my mother's family. I couldn't wait for them to leave so that we could get down to some serious business. But the ritual of tea and fruit cake had to be gone through. Then the usual small-talk of catching up with family gossip. Then … oh no! …

not holiday photos. Yes, my mother produced a folder of snaps taken on our last summer holiday in Jersey, and went through every minute detail of the trip.

"This couple we met on the beach at St. Aubin's Bay" mother explained, brandishing a somewhat well-worn black-and-white print. "Delightful, they were. He was a Jewish dentist from Westcliff-on-Sea. Very classy people. They asked the ice-cream lady if the vanilla was kosher. She didn't seem to know, but they had it anyway."

"Do we all need to know this?" I thought to myself. This was information overload gone crazy. I was getting impatient.

But at last …..

"Well, Joe, we'd better make a move. It's a long way up to Hull and we must get there before dark" my mother declared at last. *("Not before time" I thought.)* "Are you sure you'll be all right with uncle and auntie, John" she continued. "You can always phone your cousins if you're homesick and want to talk to us". *(Homesick! HOMESICK! This place is heaven, and I could stay here for the rest of my life! For goodness sake, GO!)*

And then they went.

Even as a 10-year-old, I knew that it wouldn't be polite to immediately crash in with what I considered the most important thing that had occupied my mind for the last six months. So I silently counted to ten, and then blurted out "Did you like the movie clip I sent you?"

"You were very good" came Tommy's reply "but you gave it away with your eyes. When you do the changeover in the Sub Trunk routine, you must never let the audience know there is anything else going on behind the curtain below you. Your eyes momentarily glanced down. Never do that. I'll rehearse it with you later." "Goodness, Tommy, you don't expect me to get in the trunk?" my aunt exclaimed.

"So have I passed the test?" I anxiously asked.

"Yes, I'll keep my promise" Uncle Tommy replied, and slowly got up from the chair. The same sounds could be heard coming from the kitchen as I had heard three years earlier, as the entire contents of the cupboard emptied themselves onto the kitchen floor. After much swearing and muttering, and what seemed like endless minutes, he emerged carrying the precious casket. Out came the pile of folded posters and photos, and then the beautiful key.

"Get me some paper and a pencil, Rene." It was like *déjà vu*. It was happening all over again. Auntie returned with the items he'd requested.

First, Uncle scribbled a load of completely illegible rubbish on a piece of the paper, and rolled it up tightly. He put this in the box, and showed me that hidden inside the lid was a piece of plywood which exactly matched the bottom of the box. As he closed the lid, this loose piece of wood fell down to form a false bottom to the box, completely covering the paper, so that the box looked empty. He locked the box and handed me the key.

"Take a close look at that key, boy" he said. I turned it over in my hand. It was very heavy, with a long shaft and an ornate design to its handle end, and an intricate series of grooves in the blade (the part that operates the lock) at the other end. "You remember when the newspaper landed on the doormat with the headline I'd predicted the previous day? Well, actually the paperboy had delivered the paper about two hours before, when you were still in bed. I read the headline, and wrote it on a duplicate piece of paper, rolled it up, and..."

He took the key from me, and slid a second rolled-up cylinder of paper into the open end of the hollow shaft of the key. Then, holding the handle of the key in one hand and the blade in the other, he twisted the key. There was a clicking sound as a mechanism in the key operated, and the piece of paper was fired out of the shaft of the key and onto the floor. A spring-loaded plunger in the key shaft operated just like a miniature pop-gun when the key was twisted. Even with the paper in the key, it looked completely innocent.

"When you got up, I had already written the headline onto the paper and put it in the key. After breakfast I got your aunt to nip round the outside of the cottage and push the newspaper through the letterbox. You thought it was the paperboy delivering it. We read the headline together. I gave you the key to open the box, and as you turned the key in the lock the piece of paper was fired through the lock into the apparently empty box, and there was the prediction that you thought I'd written the previous day!"

I was speechless.

I took the key and the box back from him and examined every square inch of both these treasures. The combination of cabinet maker and locksmith had produced an item of such beauty and intricacy that had provided a good living for this lovely old couple in their later performing years.

I vowed that one day I would create an original illusion myself that would baffle and amaze audiences just like this. It wasn't for another 12 years before that was to be accomplished, but I'm pleased to say my dream came true.

The rest of the week was sheer bliss. They recounted tales of their adventures touring the variety halls in the early 1900s, and of the extraordinary people and bizarre acts that they encountered. We pored over photographs, publicity bills and other memorabilia that they had kept, and I told them of the shows I had performed back home. Auntie Rene taught me some acrobatic tricks, and Uncle Tommy showed me the plans for a levitation illusion he had designed but never built. We discovered his old fire-eating props in the bottom of a trunk, but these were rapidly spirited away by auntie who said it was irresponsible for Tommy to teach a young kid of ten to eat fire!

The week flew by.

And then my parents arrived to take me home. Home to school, and homework, and cleaning the car, polishing shoes and having to eat cabbage, and all the other stuff that little boys hate.

At Christmas my parents took me to the pantomime at the Golders Green Hippodrome in North London. In one of the scenes, a spectacular cloud of low-lying fog drifted across the stage in one of the ballet scenes. How did they do that? Then in another scene everything seemed to glow in the dark ... the scenery, the costumes, the props, they all glowed! How did they do that? Then the wicked witch shot up through a trapdoor in the stage accompanied by a loud bang, flash and puff of smoke. There had to be some sort of catapult mechanism under the stage, and a firework of some type to make the bang and flash. But how? I *needed* to know.

And how did they manage to change the scenery so quickly? In the semi-darkness between two scenes, I noticed that the scenery was going upwards out of sight over the stage, and other scenery was descending to replace it. The ceiling above the stage must have been very high! It dawned on me that most of the scenery was actually dangling from ropes above the stage, and could drop down almost instantly when they did a scene change. So that's how they did it so quickly! I just had to see this for myself. Would they let me go backstage? I asked my parents if there was any chance I could get a look behind the scenes.

After the show we went round to the stage door. Within the cramped space at the foot of the stairs by the stage door-keeper's office was a chaotic world of half-dressed people, thick cigarette smoke, part-eaten sausage rolls, whicker hampers... and a strange steaming machine. It seemed to be disgorging in a rather half-hearted manner the strange heavy mist that had floated across the stage in the ballet scene I had witnessed earlier. A man appeared from a door marked "Stage - this way" and opened a flap on the top of the machine, looked inside, and asked the stage door-keeper "Eddie, has the dry ice been delivered for the second house?". Dry ice? I must find out about this.

My dad went up to the window: "My little boy has just enjoyed your pantomime and wondered if he could look around backstage?" I won't elaborate on the exact reply he got from the miserable old stage door-keeper, but it was basically: a) Who do you think you are? b) We're far too busy to waste time on little kids like him. c) Why doesn't he go home and play with his train set.

So we went home.

But I was undeterred.

I got on the phone to Uncle Tommy: "Uncle, we went to the pantomime, and all the scenery seemed to be going upwards. Are all theatres like that?" He briefly explained that above most large theatre stages was a space known as "the flies" and above that was a grid with pulleys which allowed things like scenery, curtains and lights to be suspended and winched up and down. "I'll show you some pictures when you come and see us next summer," he said.

Unfortunately, I never got to visit them the next summer, or ever again. Both Tommy and Rene died within a month of each other the following Spring.

With no reason to visit Suffolk any more, a week's holiday in Clacton-on-Sea (just down the coast) was arranged for the following summer. Our next door neighbours, Mr. & Mrs. Dadswell, had a friend who had a cousin who had a friend who had a caravan on a site at Jaywick Sands just outside Clacton, and we could rent this for the week at a special "close friends" (!) rate. My parents reluctantly made the reservation and paid what seemed a rather large sum of money up front.

The same Austin Cambridge car made the weary journey through London and up through Essex to Jaywick Sands, which we discovered to our horror was a rather sad and dreary place, with rows and rows of drab caravans interspersed with the odd fish-and-chip shop and doleful amusement arcade. Our alarm was compounded when we saw the caravan, which had the appearance of a vomit-coloured inflated beach ball, pierced only with a little door and two tiny windows. It looked as if a puff of wind could send it rolling across the site and onto the beach. The communal toilet block was filthy, the bar and cafeteria smelled the same way the caravan was coloured, and my mother decided that there was no way we were going to spend a single night there. We went off to find a suitable "bed and breakfast" in a more genteel part of town.

My memories of the lodgings we found are very vague (except for the fact that the proprietress was a dragon of a woman who had a moustache, and referred to me as "The Boy"), simply because my mind was completely assaulted by the wonders of Clacton Pier.

Nowadays, a parent would be arrested for neglect if they were to allow any child of theirs under the age of about 23 to go around unaccompanied by a responsible adult. But back in 1961 the world appeared to be a much safer place (I use the word "appeared" advisedly), and it was perfectly acceptable to allow an 11-year-old to wander around on his own. Every day I would disappear from my parent's little encampment on the beach (two deck chairs, a folding picnic table with a Fablon covered bubbly top, a Primus stove, picnic hamper, various spades and implements to build full-sized replicas of the Tower of London in sand, boxes containing tubes of suncream, Germoline, and enough medical apparatus to perform major heart surgery, etc. etc.). "Can I have some money for an icecream please?" I would ask. A half-crown coin was duly handed over, accompanied by "Don't stray far away". Four hours later I would return, and my parents would give no indication at all of having missed me, having been engrossed in the Reader's Digest and the Printer's Gazette all the time I was away.

But I had one destination in mind. The pier.

The major landmark on the pier was a huge rollercoaster called "Steel Stella". This was the biggest thing I'd ever seen at a fairground. It was indeed very impressive, with little cars that were pulled up to the highest point of the track on a chain, and then left to free-wheel back down along an undulating course under their own momentum. But a much smaller attraction next to it aroused my curiosity even more. It was an extraordinary-looking thing called "The Ghost Train" which consisted of an open-fronted windowless building with scary things painted on the outside. Little train engines that seated two people disappeared through a pair of doors at one end, and popped out a couple of minutes later from another pair of doors at the other. The occupants of these trains emerged looking either very shocked or laughing hysterically. A funny wailing sound like an air-raid siren could be heard coming from inside the building, together with an assortment of banging and crashing noises. What on earth happened inside the Ghost Train? I had to find out.

"Steel Stella" and "the Ghost Train" at Clacton Pier 1961

I paid my sixpence to the man at the entrance and climbed into the little engine. "Keep your arms and legs inside the car" warned a notice next to the doors. The man gave the car a shove, and it coasted towards the doors, crashed into them, and entered the building. It was pitch black inside. The car veered violently to the right, and then again to the left. Suddenly, out of the darkness a light came on and illuminated a skeleton in a coffin, which sat bolt upright as we passed. Then we headed straight for a wall on which had been painted a spooky face. Bash! We hit the wall, and the face melted away. Darkness once again. Something horrible tickled my face. A ghost lit up in front of me, and made the same siren wailing sound that I had heard outside the building. We swerved to miss it, and another skeleton holding an axe swung into view. A huge green octopus writhed its tentacles above us, then round another bend, and a witch on a broomstick swung towards us. Finally, crash, we hit the doors and we were back out into the daylight.

"That was amazing" I thought. But then things started to race through my mind: "How did they fit all this inside that little building?" "What made the things move just as you were going past them?" "How did the little train go around such tight corners, what steered it and what powered it?" I needed answers to all these questions. I noticed each time we turned a sharp corner in the darkness, the wheels of the engine made a loud clicking sound. And there was a motor grinding away under the seat somewhere. This was intriguing!

I walked all around the outside of the little Ghost Train building. Inside the ride, it had seemed as if we were going for miles in the darkness! Surely it couldn't have all fitted inside? Further investigation was required!

Of my two shillings and sixpence, I now had two shillings left. There was only one thing to do. Go into the town, find Woolworths, and buy a torch. Inspection by torchlight was necessary if I was to find answers to these puzzles. I needed sixpence for a second ride on the Ghost Train, so the torch couldn't cost more than one-and-six. Fortunately Woolworths was just up Pier Avenue, which was appropriately-named. Within 15 minutes I was back with my torch concealed under my pullover and ready for a second, rather more "illuminating", ride on the Ghost Train. This time I'd find out exactly how everything worked.

The final sixpence was handed over, and in I went. As soon as the doors closed behind me, out came the torch, and I flicked on the switch. Nothing. No batteries! The torch didn't come with batteries. - Stupid boy!

The next day on the beach, I made the usual request "Can I have some money for an icecream please?" The half-crown was duly handed over, accompanied by "Don't stray far away", and off I went to the pier via Woolworths for some batteries. These cost a shilling. I therefore had enough money left for three sixpenny rides on the Ghost Train. In that time I should have everything well-sussed and would be able to build my own one in the garage when we got home next week. Simple!

This third ride was very different to the two I'd had the previous day. With my torch illuminating all around, I tried to see exactly how it all worked. The trains were guided around a pitch dark room through a maze of black-painted partitions along an electrified guide rail which could turn amazingly sharp corners. The "ghosts" were rather crudely made life-size puppets that were operated by strings and pulleys. As the little car went along the track past a "ghost" it would push a spring-loaded lever to one side, which in turn pulled the strings. The metal wheels of the car ran over electric contacts on the floor which made the lights go on and off and the siren wail. The doors opened and shut simply by the train bashing into them, and springs pulling them closed. The fourth ride was used to refine my knowledge and discover that the "cobwebs" that brushed your face were actually a few lengths of disgustingly dirty string dangling from a rafter above.

The fifth ride was taken up mainly by investigating what powered the little engines around the track. Once safely inside, out came the torch, and I discovered that the seat I was sitting on could hinge up to reveal the mechanism under it. An electric motor turned the rear axle of the vehicle via a chain and sprockets. As the car turned a sharp bend, the inside wheel on the bend would stay almost stationary, whilst the outside wheel made a loud clicking sound (a crude "differential", as I was later to discover). The front of the car had no wheels, but rested on a grooved guide roller on the track.

My mind was still racing as we emerged back out into the sunlight ...... "Could I convert a broken wheelbarrow, some metal pipes, an old car seat ......"

I was going to build my own Ghost Train. And I would charge sixpence a go!

Chapter 3

THE CAREER AHEAD

At the end of the holidays I started at a new secondary school and the Ghost Train building project had to be put on hold.

The new school was a daunting experience, as the masters wore gowns and mortar boards, and addressed you by your surname. You had to learn Latin, and sang weird songs, and had to call the prefects "Sir". And they didn't call dinner "dinner". They called it "lunch".

But it had a stage ... with curtains, and lights. Did it have the high ceiling that all stages are supposed to have, where you hung the scenery and things? No, it didn't, but there had to be other ways to ...

My thoughts were starting to race already.

One day when I came down to breakfast my father was beaming as he read a letter that had arrived in the post that morning. With great pride, he handed it across the breakfast table. It was from the Principal of the London College of Printing. It read:

Dear Mr. Wardley,

With reference to your letter dated 17th. October 1961, I have pleasure in confirming that it is the policy of the London College of Printing to give priority to the sons of Members of the Guild of Master Printers when allocating places on our courses. To this end, although your son will not be eligible for admission to the College for another seven years, I will be pleased to allocate a place for him provisionally, subject to him reaching the necessary scholastic standards in the General Certificate of Education Examinations.

Yours sincerely,

J.R. Riddell

(Principal)

Tears started to well up in my eyes.

"Is something wrong, John?" my mother asked. I ran out of the room, grabbed my school bag and coat, and shot out of the front door.

When I got home that evening from school, my father had still not returned from his day at the office. "That letter, this morning" my mother said, "you didn't seem very happy about it. You know your father wants you to go into the family business. You do want to, don't you?"

I loved my father very much, and the last thing I wanted to do was be a disappointment to him. Five generations of Wardleys had built up the family business, and I was expected to perpetuate the enterprise. But I blurted out: "I want to work in the theatre. Not posh theatre like Shakespeare and stuff. Fun theatre like Uncle Tommy and Auntie Rene used to do. And magic. And circuses. And things like they had on Clacton Pier last year like Ghost Trains and shows."

"Well that's all very well for some kinds of people" (my mother had refrained from using the word "common", but that's what she meant) "but your father and I are sacrificing a lot to give you a good education, and we want you to use it properly."

"But every working day, dad puts on his boring old suit, takes the same boring old train up to Moorgate, sits in his boring old office, and does the same boring old things. He'll never have the same fun stories to tell as uncle and auntie had. They had a happy life. I'll never have that if I become a printer."

Although my mother never said anything more, I knew that deep down she understood exactly where I was coming from. But how could I win over my father without hurting him. Ironically, and unintentionally, he was to do that himself a few years later.

Out of respect (and gratitude) to my parents I worked hard at school, and chose science subjects for "O" level GCEs. But I became stage manager for the school plays, helped construct the scenery for the local amateur dramatic society, and made a decent little income performing my magic act for local shows.

On my twelfth birthday, I came down to breakfast and an intriguing-looking present was waiting for me, wrapped in colourful "Happy Birthday" paper. I opened it, and found inside a strange metal object with my name beautifully engraved on the underside of it. It was shaped like a long narrow tray, open along one edge, with a sliding piece that could move across the whole length and a lever to lock it in any position. My father was beaming with pride. "Do you like it?" he said. "Yes, but what is it?" I asked. "It's your very own composing stick" he replied.

In case you are wondering what a composing stick is (and I certainly was on that birthday morning) here is the dictionary definition:-

> "In letterpress printing and typesetting, a composing stick is an instrument used to assemble pieces of metal type into words and lines which are later bound into a forme, set in a galley and printed. The compositor takes the letter blocks from the compartments of the type case and places them in the composing stick, working from left to right and placing the letters upside down with the nick to the top."

My father continued: "It is a tradition handed down from your great-grandfather to your grandfather, and from your grandfather to me. We were all given our own composing stick at the age of twelve to signify our future entry into our trade. Keeping up with the tradition, this is yours, and I will teach you how to use it."

This was the most miserable birthday present anyone could have been given. But I tried not to show it. From then on, every Saturday morning I would be taken by my father on the train up to his printing works in Finsbury Square (by this time they'd moved from George Street), London, and spend interminable hours practising putting the little metal letters into the composing stick, transferring them to the galley, locking them in place, putting it in the printing press, and printing a single sheet of paper (which my father would look over with critical pride). I was given texts of Masefield poetry, tables of meteorological data, newspaper articles and all sorts of other mundane things to turn into set type and then print.

My thirteenth birthday was a considerably happier occasion. I had been asked what I'd like to do to celebrate, and said I wanted to go to Battersea Funfair. I had caught a glimpse of this magical place when my mother had taken me to the Festival Gardens in Battersea Park several years before, but had not been allowed to go into the funfair as "it wasn't a very nice place for children to go" as my mum put it. It turned out that it was a VERY nice place for children to go! At least, for children like me with an insatiable curiosity for that sort of thing.

So it was arranged that my schoolmate Stephen Jenkins and I would go to the funfair in the afternoon, and then move on to the Lyons Corner House in the Strand in central London to meet my parents for a birthday meal. It was a complicated train and bus journey to Battersea Park, but as soon as we arrived it became apparent to us that we had to inspect every single square inch of the place. The Big Dipper was the dominant ride, and was enjoyable but not particularly inspiring. Underneath it was the Haunted Goldmine, which was a themed ghost train, and, since I was an expert on ghost trains by now (!), I bored poor Stephen Jenkins to death going on about how it all worked. The Crazy Cottage was great fun. It was a little two-storey cottage built on an alarming tilt, so that you fell about and lost your balance as you staggered through its passageways.

The World Cruise was interesting. It took you through a series of grottos in little boats, from which you viewed static tableaux of various scenes from around the world. The attraction was rather dull and boring, made interesting only by the fact that previous bored voyagers had obviously got out of their boats and "rearranged" some of the figures in the tableaux. Even a 13 year-old knew that the penguins in Antarctica couldn't possibly pro-create in the incredible positions into which they had been rearranged. But it was the way the boats floated along propelled by the current of water that intrigued me. There appeared to be a constant gentle slope to the trough of water to make the current flow, and after you got out of your boat in the station at the end of the ride, the boat went up a short conveyor belt and was deposited back at the start of the ride about two feet higher up, whilst a large waterwheel lifted the water up to this point. "Hmmm. Must bear this in mind" I thought.

Just inside the main entrance to the funfair was a booth that proclaimed "See the Invisible Man!". (This seemed a bit of a misnomer… if he were really invisible, how could you see him?) Outside was a microphone on a stand, which was moving as if being held by the invisible man. The recorded voice promised that if we ventured inside, one of us would be chosen to be blasted with a newly-discovered atomic ray which would turn you invisible. We just had to go in! We paid our sixpences. Inside the crowded booth (which stank of a million sweaty bodies) was a small stage on which stood a strange-looking machine. Someone from the audience was volunteered to go up on stage and entered the machine via a door in the back. The machine had a glass front, and the man could be clearly seen in its illuminated interior.

The showman held up a small hand-mirror in front of the box and asked the man inside "Can you see this mirror?". "Yes," came the reply from within. "Can you see yourself in the mirror?" Again, "Yes," was the reply. "I will now switch on the atomic ray". The showman moved to the impressive-looking control panel and started to operate its knobs and switches. There was a loud humming sound of high voltage electricity and lights started to flash. Then slowly the man inside the machine began to become transparent. We could clearly see the back of the machine behind him through his body. Eventually he was completely invisible. The showman repeated the procedure with the mirror: "Can you see this mirror?" ... "Yes," came the reply. "Now, can you see yourself in the mirror?" ... "No!" With great pride the showman turned to the audience and said "Ladies and gentleman, he can see the mirror, but he can't see his own reflection. He has TRULY become invisible!"

Although the audience were probably rather impressed and totally baffled by what they had seen, the round of applause was rather half-hearted, but Stephen and I enthusiastically showed our appreciation and wonderment. We left the booth thrilled and perplexed.

On the other side of the building was a smaller sideshow, which promised within "The Amazing Spider Girl – the head of a beautiful young lady with the body of a giant spider – Alive! Living! Breathing! Talking!". The façade was adorned with a mural depicting a huge hairy spider on a web, but with the head and face of a rather glamorous-looking girl.

Now in the house where we lived, giant spiders with lady's heads were few and far between. So we paid our sixpence and in we went. This time the booth was almost empty save for a young boy and girl whose lips seemed to be permanently superglued together throughout the performance we were about to witness. In the corner of the booth, which was decorated with cheap plastic foliage to resemble a tropical jungle, the showman pulled aside a curtain to reveal an arrangement of tree branches, stretched across which was a huge artificial spider's web. In the centre of this web was a girl's head, with a small spider's body attached. The girl appeared to have no body of her own. The effect of her being "Alive! Living! Breathing! Talking!" was achieved by her constantly chewing gum, and looking thoroughly bored to tears. "It's got to be a dummy head" Stephen muttered. "No, I think she must be deformed in some way" I responded. This provoked a vocal response from the spider that indignantly announced "I'm not f@©king deformed, you little pr%©ks." Then the spider carried on chewing her gum and asked the attendant to get her a Mars Bar.

I was determined by hook or by crook to find out how this worked. I noticed some playful customer had thrown an empty chip tray at the spider (no wonder the poor girl didn't look as if she enjoyed her job), and it was lying on the artificial grass mat beneath the web. But an identical chip tray was also to be seen, complete with the same smudges of ketchup, on the grass *behind* the web. This was too much of a coincidence. One must be a reflection of the other in a mirror. When I got home, I bought an old dressing table mirror from a jumble sale, and experimented with it. Soon I had my own portable version of the Amazing Spider Girl that I took to local fetes and bazaars. ("Mrs. Watson, is Sheila free for a few hours next Saturday?").

The one thing that disappointed me about Battersea Funfair was that many of the rides in the centre of the amusement park were in fact conventional travelling fairground rides such as Waltzers, Dodgems, Speedway Arks and so on. Why would anyone travel a long distance from their home only to find virtually the same rides that had visited their local village green a few weeks previously? I was later to discover that the more enlightened amusement parks such as Blackpool Pleasure Beach would share this view, and, wherever possible, would try to create unique and special attractions. And I maintain this opinion that I had formed at the age of 13 to the present day. (In Battersea Funfair's defence, the park was initially developed in a great hurry after the end of the Second World War as part of the Festival of Britain, but that is no excuse for many other permanent amusement parks around the country.)

Stephen and I continued to explore the delights of most of the rides and attractions until I suddenly noticed the time. It was six-o'clock, and we were due to meet my parents in the "Brasserie" of the Lyons Corner House in the Strand, next to Charing Cross Station, at six-thirty. We ran out of the funfair towards Chelsea Bridge. We didn't know if a bus went in the direction of Trafalgar Square, there was no nearby tube station, and we didn't have enough money (or the *savoir faire*) to hail a taxi. There was nothing for it but to run. We covered the three miles in less than half an hour ... along the Chelsea Embankment and Millbank, round Parliament Square Westminster, up Whitehall, across Trafalgar Square, past Charing Cross Station, and arrived in the basement "Brasserie" restaurant puffing and sweating, just in time to see my parents being shown to our table by the head waiter (to whom they had explained that they were meeting their young son, whose birthday celebration this was).

Stephen and I, disheveled and looking very out-of-place amongst the formally-dressed diners, ran across the restaurant and joined them. "Have you had a good time, boys?" my mother asked, and we launched into a rapid and detailed description of all that we had seen. The restaurant was decorated in a sort of Spanish style, and a little gypsy band played jolly music on a raised platform under one of the plaster arches. This band was lead by a giantess of a woman violinist, who must have been at least seven feet tall and built like a leading lady in a Wagnerian opera. She wore a colourful flowing gypsy costume and pendulous gold hooped rings dangled from her ears. Her ample bosom allowed her to balance her violin on her chest without any other visible means of support, thereby allowing her both hands free to conduct the band when she wasn't playing her instrument. Stephen and I exchanged some very silly and juvenile jokes about why the restaurant was called a "Brasserie", and were told by my mother to behave.

After the main course, I felt the need for a pee (we had consumed large quantities of fizzy drinks at the funfair, and the mad dash to the restaurant had left no time for this before we arrived). I excused myself from the table, and made for the toilets. As I was relieving myself in the relative tranquility of the gents, I could hear the gypsy band strike up "Happy Birthday". I finished what I was doing and exited the toilet door back into the restaurant to discover to my horror that in my absence the gypsy band had formed a procession, lead by the head waiter, and was making for our table. The head waiter was carrying a birthday cake ablaze with lighted candles, and all the diners around the restaurant were watching in rapt attention. I froze on the spot. The cake was put down in front of Stephen who was looking alarmed and embarrassed. "No, no!" my dad shouted. "It's not HIS birthday." The gypsy band stopped playing mid-verse in a rather hap-hazard manner (rather like an old gramophone record running down). "No," Stephen shouted in the deafening silence that resulted. "John's gone to have a pee!" and pointed across the restaurant to the toilet door outside which I stood. The giantess violinist glared ominously at me, and all eyes in the room followed her. The head waiter furiously extinguished the candles, and the motley procession made its way back to the kitchen. The birthday cake never returned.

I continued to go to my father's printing works on Saturdays for the next couple of years, but gradually my father began to realise that my heart wasn't really in it. So, unbeknown to me, he was hatching a cunning plan to win me over to join the family business. His accountant had another client called Jack Jay who owned a chain of theatres, bingo halls and other entertainment operations around the east coast seaside resorts. My father phoned him up, and the conversation must have gone something like this:

> "Jack, my lad has got it into his head that he wants to work in show business. It's only a passing fad, and he'll be much more secure coming into our printing firm. If I send him to you during his school summer holidays to work for you, could you give him all the shitty jobs you can think of, and knock this stage-struck nonsense out of his head once and for all?"

Jack (or "Mr. Jay" as I was to always call him) obviously said he'd oblige.

So, in the summer of 1966 after I had done my "O" level exams my father asked me if I'd like to spend my school holidays working at the Windmill Theatre in Great Yarmouth for a friend of his who owned it. I should have smelled a rat, but I was so surprised and delighted, I said "You bet!".

A couple of weeks later I was bundled off on the train with my bike from Liverpool Street Station in London, and told to go to my lodgings with a Miss Bond, at 5 Hammond Road, Northgate Street, Great Yarmouth. And then be at the Windmill Theatre on the seafront for 9:30 the following morning and report to Mr. Rayner, the theatre manager.

I found my lodgings quite easily. It was a nice little terraced house in a quiet side street, and I immediately liked Miss Bond (I never found out her Christian name - perhaps she never had one). She was tall and thin. I was 16 and she was 74. But she had a wonderful sense of humour, and we developed a very good rapport. She kept the house spotlessly clean, and provided full board and lodging with three good cooked meals a day plus supper after the evening show, all for seven guineas a week (that's £7.35 a week).

"There's loads of show people living around this part of town for the summer" she said in her delightful broad Norfolk accent shortly after I arrived. "Ruby Murray is with Mrs Harrison in Kitchener Road, and that midget is renting a posh house in Wellesley Road". (It turned out that "that midget" was actually Jimmy Clitheroe, a famous comedian of the time.) You've got Ruby Murray in your show at the Windmill, I think," she continued "And Freddie and the Dreamers. I don't know where they're staying."

Miss Bond was the complete antithesis of the stereotypical theatrical landlady. She was kind, fun, and provided me with every home comfort. So far, so good.

The following morning I set off on my bike along Great Yarmouth's promenade for the Windmill Theatre. Even with my eyes closed, I can always tell when I'm on Yarmouth's Golden Mile. It is the smell. A combination of horse poo (from the horse-drawn carriages that take holidaymakers on rides along the prom.), candyfloss, vinegar and fish, peppered occasionally by that strange electric-sparking smell that comes from funfair dodgem car rides. It might not sound like a perfect odour, but to me it's a perfume that brings back memories of that idyllic hot summer of 1966.

You couldn't miss the Windmill Theatre, with its landmark revolving illuminated sails adorning the façade, and the giant photo-realistic cutout faces of the stars of the show within. I chained my bike to the "No Parking" sign outside, and went up to the box office. The lady behind the window had a big bouffant hair-do nearly as tall as herself. She looked kindly at me. "I'm here to see Mr. Rayner. My name's John Wardley". She disappeared through a door, and a few moments later the theatre manager, Bob Rayner appeared. He was a very impressive-looking gentleman in a smart tuxedo (he always wore a tuxedo, no matter what time of day, or what he was doing) with a Clark Gable moustache and dark wavy Brylcreemed hair.

Given that I was the son of a friend of the boss, it would have been easy for Mr. Rayner to have looked on me with disdain. In theory I was some stagestruck lad with stars in his eyes who had no idea of the real facts of showbiz life, dumped on the theatre to keep him amused during the summer holidays. But, instead Mr Rayner and his staff treated me with kindness and respect. They did work me hard, though. VERY hard. I was going to be put to the test.

I was told that the show ("The Freddie and the Dreamers Show with full supporting cast") ran twice nightly, with additional afternoon matinees on Thursdays and Saturdays. I would be working as a stagehand

(and general dogsbody) backstage at the show. I also had to be at the theatre for 9:30 every day except Sundays to work the morning and afternoon bingo sessions. After the show at night I had to report to the Empire Cinema along the promenade to help the projectionist re-wind the day's films. In theory, I would have Sunday mornings off, but I would be expected to do some fly-posting of posters around the town on my bike during that time. I would then do Sunday afternoon and evening bingo sessions.

What had I let myself in for?

I had never been in a cash bingo hall before, but the daytime use of the theatre for this purpose was a real money-spinner for Jack Jay, and many of the show people earned extra money in the daytime working the bingo. Nobby Phelps the stage manager was the bingo caller, and most of the backstage staff sold bingo cards or checked numbers. It made for a very long working day, but for the twelve week summer season it was tolerable and lucrative for them.

On my first day I was told to watch what happened, because the next day I would be put on ticket sales. The speed with which things proceeded was alarming. In just half an hour before each session, the audience of 500 people would have to be sold a very complicated array of different tickets for various games, and each player had their own demands on how they wanted the tickets sequentially arranged ("I want eight National Golden Scoop cards, two doubles, one treble and a single out of sequence"). The individual tickets, which came on perforated strips, were priced at very awkward amounts in the old currency of pounds, shillings, and pence, so you had to do a very quick mental calculation to compute that eight tickets at 1s 4d each (one shilling and four pence each) would cost a total of 10s 8d (there were 12 pence to a shilling, and 20 shillings to the pound). If the player gave you a one pound note, that required 9s 4d change. Each customer had to be served in just a few seconds, and they then moved on to the next seller along the line for the tickets for the next game. The cost of any tickets you had left over out of sequence was deducted from your wages at the end of the week.

Once the games had started, you were positioned strategically around the audience to check the ticket of any player who claimed a win.

Although it might appear mundane, the work was actually great fun, and had considerable perks when you convinced a player that you had brought them luck by selling them that particular ticket, and they tipped you handsomely from their winnings. The other perk was that I always was stationed along the selling line next to Rose Gerrard. Rose was undoubtedly (in my juvenile opinion) the most beautiful girl in the world. She had been Miss Feltham Carnival Queen, and was gorgeous. In the evening, she was an usherette in the theatre and sold programmes. It was the year of Flower Power, and she used to wear a flower in her hair and a little bell on a chain round her neck. She allowed me on numerous occasions that summer to ring her bell.

That evening I arrived at the stage door at about 5:30 and met Nobby the stage manager, whom I'd already met as bingo caller during the day. He took me across the stage into the wings where the old Grand Master lighting switchboard was located, and introduced me to Freddy Kent, the lighting man. Far from being annoyed at having an ignorant kid seconded to him, he seemed quite relieved. Today, stage lighting control boards are sophisticated computer-controlled affairs with presets and memories. But way back in 1966 there was no such technology. The giant mechanical monster of a switchboard consisted of huge levers which could be latched onto rotating shafts, thereby allowing individual dimmers to be preset to move in synchronisation when the relevant cue was given to change the lighting pattern onstage. Some of the cues in the show needed an octopus to manipulate the levers, and he was very grateful for an extra pair of hands, even if they belonged to a complete novice. My enthusiasm to do it right was matched by an aptitude for the job, and we very quickly worked as a team and I was accepted as a valuable part of the crew.

The show itself was a variety bill, with dance numbers, singers, comedians and novelty acts. Freddie and the Dreamers topped the bill, and the show ended with a spectacular number involving Ultra Violet lighting (so that's how things glowed in the dark at the Golders Green Hippodrome Pantomime!) and fountains (which leaked all over the stage). My final job when the curtain came down was to mop the stage and top up the fountain tank with a bucket of water ready for the next performance. (Apparently, my predecessor had put a squirt of Fairy Liquid in the water as a prank the previous week, and had been sacked after a mountain of foam oozed across the stage in the Grand Finale, causing three of the female dancers to perform unchoreographed splits in their routine).

After the second performance of the show ended at about 10:30 in the evening, it was back on my bike and down the prom to the Empire

Cinema to help the projectionist rewind the films. Nowadays cinema projection rooms are clinically clean hi-tech environments, but the Empire's was nothing of the sort and looked (and stank) like a miniature iron smelting works. The massive projectors burned carbon arc lamps which produced a thick black dust which seemed to cover everything. The poor lad who was the projectionist appeared to live in this prison 24 hours a day, and his pallid complexion indicated that he never saw the sunlight (and his diet of Tizer, Walker's Potato Puffs, and Milky Bars garnished it with acne boils). He worked entirely alone, without an assistant, so that by the end of the day he was surrounded by a chaotic pile of overflowing reels of film that needed sorting out and rewinding for the following day. This could take anything from ten minutes (if everything went according to plan) to two hours (if a film had broken or a projector had jammed and spewed film onto the floor).

Next to one of the projectors were two small buttons marked "OPEN" and "CLOSE", which controlled the curtains at the screen (why don't modern multiplex cinemas have curtains anymore?). I asked Stuart, the projectionist, if I could see the motor that worked the curtains. "There's no motor" he replied. "The buttons ring a bell in the icecream fridge room, to tell one of the usherettes to go backstage and pull on the curtain ropes".

I never got back to Hammond Road till at least 2am, and my supper, consisting of a freshly-cut ham sandwich and half a cup of milk in a saucepan to heat up with some Camp Coffee essence, was waiting for me. It was not for several weeks that I discovered Miss Bond always put out a full cup of milk in the saucepan, but by the time I got back the cat had drunk half of it.

Six days a week this pattern was repeated, starting work at 9:30 and finishing around 1 or 2 in the morning. But I was 16, healthy, and loved every minute. It didn't seem like work to me.

Sundays meant a lie-in until at least 9 o'clock.

Have you ever seen anyone fly-posting bills? No, I bet you haven't. Fly-posters have developed an amazing technique that allows them to move through a town totally invisibly. Now, fly-posting is illegal, and can be classed as vandalism. But in Great Yarmouth there was an unwritten understanding that the various charity showbiz events that took place around the town during the summer season could advertise themselves in this maverick way. Jack Jay was about to become Chief

Barker of the Variety Club of Great Britain in two years time, and was heavily involved in organizing the celebrity football matches, golf tournaments, midnight charity matinees and other fund-raising events. And I was the person delegated to "papering" (as the activity is colloquially known) the town to advertise them. The rules were simple:

        1)   Never post on a "virgin" site. (In other words, only post over another obsolete or defaced bill)

        2)   Never post over someone else's current poster (i.e. only post on old, out of date bills)

        3)   Do it as quickly and unobtrusively as possible, and disappear immediately afterwards.

I developed a highly effective technique. I would cycle round town looking for suitable sites, with a bucket of paste dangling from the handlebars of my bike and a roll of DayGlo bills in my saddlebag. When I found a site, in a flash, I would have a bill face down on the wall, the paste brush would be a blur as it smeared the back with paste, the bill was peeled off and folded in three, and then turned around, unfolded, and placed in position. A quick over-paste on the front, and I was back on the bike and mingling with the traffic. My technique was sheer poetry-in-motion.

In fact this cloak-and-dagger technique was totally unnecessary, as everyone in the town welcomed these charity events that helped under-privileged and handicapped children all over the country, and their advertisement in this way was welcomed. But it made the job much more fun!

One Sunday, I ran out of posters. A quick phone call to Mr. Jay, and it was arranged that I could go to the poster printers to collect some more bills.

Rex Studios was the company that produced the DayGlo posters for the shows, and also the scenery, signs and the giant 8 ft. high cut-out faces of the stars that adorned all the theatres in Great Yarmouth. This was in the days long before digital photography and printing, and each face was hand-reproduced from actual photos using airbrushes. It was an amazingly skillful art.

As it was a Sunday, and the Studio was closed, it had been arranged that a young signwriter's apprentice called Bruce would meet me at the Studio at 11 o'clock and hand over the posters to me. I set off on my bike to the southern end of Great Yarmouth and found Rex Studios in a maze of warehouses and industrial units just a few streets back from the Pleasure Beach amusement park. I banged on the roller-shutter door, and a young lad a couple of years older than me appeared carrying the posters. We struck up a conversation and I asked him how they painted the giant portraits for the theatre fronts.

Bruce took me inside the deserted studio, which was an Aladdin's cave of half-painted scenery and signs. On an easel in one corner was a small photo of Engelbert Humperdinck onto which a little grid of pencil lines had been drawn. Fixed to a large framework on the wall was a huge sheet of plywood, with a similar grid of lines drawn, but 20 times larger. By comparing how the details of the photo crossed the small grid, the artist was able to hand draw the same details on the plywood grid.

Bruce started-up an air compressor across the workshop, filled a small spraygun with grey paint, and with incredible speed and precision started to copy the photo onto the plywood. Within five minutes a credible likeness of Engelbert Humperdinck had started to materialize before my eyes. The lad was a genius, and would definitely go far!

It was another 25 years before our paths would cross again, and I would discover just how far this lad had gone. And we, and our respective families, would become the greatest of friends.

Chapter 4

THE CUNNING PLAN BACKFIRES

My days at the Windmill Theatre that summer were some of the happiest days of my life.

One evening during the show, I was standing in the wings on our side of the stage, and the Tornadoes were performing their old number one hit 'Telstar', when I looked across into the darkness and gloom of the wings on the other side and I thought I caught a brief glimpse of my father. No, I must be mistaken - it couldn't have been him. He was back home 150 miles away. And then the apparition went, and I forgot all about it.

It was not until many weeks later after I had got home that a story started to unfold.

It turned out that Jack Jay had realised that I was not only thoroughly enjoying the hard graft that he was putting me through, but that I had a real aptitude for the work and for the entertainment industry in general. He had phoned up my father and told him.

"I need to come up and see this for myself" my father had said. So, unbeknown to me, he came to Great Yarmouth one day, met up with Jack Jay, and watched me at work from a distance.

Mr. Jay later told me that my father had said to him, "I've lost him, Jack, haven't I?"

Jack explained to my dad that in 1968 he was going to be the Chief Barker of the Variety Club of Great Britain, which involved organizing the same charity events I had been fly-posting for that summer. If my father could resign himself to me not going into the family profession, and instead make a career in the entertainment business, then after I had completed my "A" levels in two years' time, Mr. Jay would organise for me a more carefully-structured "apprenticeship" in the various entertainment operations around Great Yarmouth.

In addition, I could also be his personal assistant helping organise and publicise the charity events. I would spend a week as a ringboy at the Hippodrome Circus, a week as a flyman in the theatre on the Wellington Pier, and a few days as a croupier at the Casino. He would arrange for me to work at the Pleasure Beach, in the box office at the Britannia Pier, in the Model Village maintenance department, at the Empire Cinema, the Windmill Theatre and at the Aquarium Nightclub. It would be the finest all round showbusiness training anyone would wish for.

Dad said he'd talk to me about it when I was back home.

And so he did.

"Your mother and I need to have a serious talk with you" my father said to me one evening, with a very grave expression on his face. He explained exactly what had happened during his covert meeting with Jack Jay. "Obviously, your heart isn't in the printing business. You really want to go into show business, don't you? But do us a favour .... Whatever you do, DO IT PROPERLY. Go to college, get some qualifications, use the education you have been given, so you can build a proper career."

"What exactly do you want to do, John?" interjected my mother,

"I want to be a stage manager in the theatre," I doggedly replied.

"Well, find out if there are any colleges that do courses in that sort of thing after you leave school," dad went on. " And take advantage of what Mr. Jay is offering you. But first, you must complete your "A" levels".

I got up and hugged both my parents. The heavy load of "Wiggins & Wardley, established 1874" was lifted from my shoulders for ever.

I entered the sixth form at school, and embarked on GCE "A" level courses in maths, physics and chemistry. The three subjects were taught by masters who got my tremendous respect, each for very different reasons.

The maths course was taught, initially, by a funny little Canadian man by the name of Rossman. He had just arrived in England, and believed that the way to teach maths was to allow the pupils to explore the numerical wonders of mathematics and make discoveries for themselves. He was there on the sidelines to help if necessary. To start off with we thought this was great fun. We were never criticized, we were allowed to get things wrong, and work out for ourselves how to correct them. But after the first term, it dawned on most of us that we were learning virtually nothing. In five terms' time we would be doing our "A" levels, and a very rigid syllabus had to be learned in order to pass the exams. By the end of the second term we were getting very concerned. So we did something rather unheard-of for a class of 16-year old boys; we held a "council of war", had a meeting with the headmaster, and got the teacher sacked.

We had wasted two terms of a five term course. The deputy headmaster and head of mathematics was a delightful old gentleman called Mr. Cummings (affectionately known by the nickname of "Joey", although that probably wasn't his actual Christian name). He was about to retire at the end of the school year, and was of the old-school type of master ... strict, but fair.

After Mr. Rossman's rapid departure, a very worried-looking Mr. Cummings addressed our class. "Boys, your school has let you down badly. We owe it to you all to get you through your "A" levels somehow. I am prepared to delay my retirement until after your exams, and I will do anything and everything you need to prepare you properly in the short time we have. I am happy to work after school hours with you, individually, or as a group. I will give you my home telephone number if you have any queries at weekends that you want to discuss. But first, I have to have an undertaking from you ... all of you ... that you are prepared to do your part. Are you with me?". To a boy, the response was: "Yes, sir!"

For the next three terms a wonderful and very respectful bond developed between that class of 18 boys and our elderly teacher. The result was the best set of "A" level maths results the school had known.

My respect for our physics master was very different but equally high. Mr. Boreham was a large ginger-haired young rugby player, straight out of university. He hadn't got a clue about how to teach or control a class of pubescent lads (even though he'd only recently been one himself) but he threw himself into the task of getting us through the "A" level syllabus with chaotic gusto.

When he heard of my ambitions to become a stage manager, I found that questions appeared in our class tests such as, "A piece of stage scenery weighing 230 lbs. is suspended from two cables each at 18 degrees to the vertical. If it is to be raised at a velocity of 3ft. per second, what power of electric motor is required to achieve this?". What he lacked in conventional teaching skills he made up for in his enthusiasm for his subject, and his desire to make this relevant to the real world and of our future careers.

Our chemistry master was called Mr. Borrows, who bore an uncanny resemblance to the (then) pop star Manfred Mann. (For this reason he was always known by the nickname "Manfred"). It turned out that his girlfriend was an actress. He was a good teacher, and made chemistry fun. He showed me how to mix titanium garniture with saltpeter to make the amazing flash of sparks, puff of smoke, and loud bang which had accompanied the appearance of the Wicked Witch on the stage of the Golders Green Hippodrome many years earlier. Again, he tried to give his subject relevance to my aspired future career path.

When my parents had asked me what sort of college course I should take to qualify as a stage manager I asked his advice, and he said he'd arrange for me to meet his girlfriend. She was a lovely lady, who was very encouraging and explained a possible route I should consider taking.

At that time, the West End theatre was dominated by shows produced by a production company called "Theatre Projects Ltd." run by a highly-respected entrepreneur, Richard Pilbrow. At any one time in the mid- to late-Sixties, at least four of the big musicals in London were his. He was concerned that the calibre of stage technicians was not matching the increasingly sophisticated technology which was starting to appear in the live theatre. "The Four Musketeers" at the Theatre Royal Drury Lane was about to open, and Sean Kenny's amazing set design required complicated hydraulic stage machinery.

Lighting control systems were utilizing solid-state electronics and very complex pre-settable operator's control boards. Multi-track sound systems with high quality amplification and sophisticated mixing desks were in increasing use. Shows were becoming very demanding in the way stage managers had to do the split-second cueing of the numerous movements of actors, scenery, sound and lighting changes. And he felt that no existing college course was producing a new generation of stage management and theatre technicians who were up to these new challenges. So he set about devising and sponsoring his own course in conjunction with one of Britain's most prestigious drama schools, the London Academy of Music and Dramatic Art (LAMDA).

I made enquiries, and discovered that applications for the course starting in September 1968 (after I had completed my school "A" levels) would be accepted from November 1967. In the intervening summer holidays whilst revising for the forthcoming exams, I made a short holiday back in Great Yarmouth to visit my old friends, then it was back home to revise.

I returned to school in September 1967 to complete the final year of my "A" level GCE courses, but applied to LAMDA for a place on their "Theatre Projects Stage Management and Technical Theatre" course for the September of the following year. I sent off the application letter, and received a response saying that I would be called for "audition" (AUDITION!!!!!) in the Spring.

Sure enough, the following April, just when I was in the thick of revising for my exams, I received a letter asking me to attend an "audition" (these theatrical types don't like to use the word "interview" ... that's far too commercial!) the following Thursday at the college in Earl's Court, London. One of the duties of a stage manager is to organise and run the audition process when casting a new show, so when I arrived everything was being done by the previous year's stage management students as work experience, checking our credentials, keeping us at ease in the waiting room, and eventually ushering us into the audition room.

Finally the time came when I was shown into a room where three very serious-looking gentlemen were seated behind a desk. One was David Chivers, a Director of Theatre Projects Trust Ltd. (who funded the course), the second was Brian Benn the course's technical director, and the third was Robert Stanton LAMDA's course administrator. These three gentlemen, I was later to discover, knew more about the backstage workings of West End theatres than the rest of the industry put together.

After the initial pleasantries, ("Why do you want to be a stage manager?" etc.) they started to probe me to draw out the usual naïve responses they got from most candidates regarding the more glamorous aspirations that the uninitiated candidates might have about the "luvvy" side of the theatre. When I started to tell them about wrestling with the levers on the old Windmill Theatre lighting switchboard, getting blisters on my hands from pulling on the fly ropes to haul up the scenery, mopping the stage from the overflowing fountain, and so on, the interviewers (sorry, "auditioners") realised that here was a candidate who didn't have his head in the clouds, and understood the hard graft that lay ahead in a career in stage management.

From that moment on the atmosphere in the room changed, we chatted like old friends and exchanged backstage tales, and I was fairly confident that I'd got a place on the course. And, as it turned out, I had.

At this point in time I had just one passionate and all-consuming goal in my life ... to pass my exams, put school behind me, go to college, and then start work as an ENTERTAINER. An entertainer seldom seen, an entertainer in the shadows, an entertainer who puts others in the limelight, but who deep down knows that the laughter, the gasps, the screams and the applause of the audience are partly of his making.

Back in school, I focused my attention on the A-level exams, which came and went, and I passed with sufficiently high grades for the local education authority to provide me with a grant for my fees for LAMDA, together with travelling- and living-expenses. I was out of my parent's pockets at last.

But before starting college there was the exciting prospect of another summer in Great Yarmouth.

Chapter 5

THE ALL-ROUND ENTERTAINER

That second summer season in Great Yarmouth was so jam-packed with experiences my mind reels trying to recall them.

Jack Jay was true to his word. The respect in which he was held by the Great and the Good in the entertainment industry, not just in East Anglia, but throughout Britain, meant that he could pull strings and get me into places where others could not tread. A phonecall from Jack (sorry, Mr. Jay, as I always called him) and doors opened.

My first week was spent as a ringboy at Billy Russell's Hippodrome Circus. Ten years later Jack's own son Peter was to take over this fantastic operation, but in 1968 it was owned and run by a very quiet and retiring gentleman ("gentleman" in the true sense of the word) called Ben Dean. When I was first introduced to him I thought he must be an accountant or bank manager, but I was later to discover all the magic that the audiences witnessed in that sawdust ring were as a result of his incredible flair and backstage dynamism. There was something to be learned from this.

The main task of the ringboys was to act as assistants to the ringmaster, rolling and unrolling the ring-mat after the animal acts, pulling on the ropes to raise and lower the trapezes, and to set and dismantle the props in the ring for the various acts.

The show opened with a parade of all the performers, followed by a bareback horse riding act. My first job was to help unfold the ring-mat as quickly as possible, whilst some clowns distracted the audience. The next item was an aerial trapeze act, where a miniature flying saucer would apparently float into the middle of the ring (it was actually on wheels) on a cloud of dry ice. The ringboys would attach cables to it, and it would be winched high up into the rigging above the circus ring. A small trapdoor would then open in the underside of the flying saucer and a trapeze would drop down from this. Then a lovely young lady emerged from the trapdoor, followed by her handsome male partner. The two would then perform an aerial acrobatic routine on the trapeze. Obviously, in order for the two performers to emerge from the flying saucer, they had to get in it in the first place backstage out of sight of the audience. Since the trapdoor was on the underneath of this little vehicle, it was necessary to tip it on its side in order for them to get in, and then lower it back to the ground. My job was to help them do this.

The performing budgerigar act required numerous tables containing miniature see-saws, swings and other novelty devices to be set in the ring with considerable precision. Things never went according to plan, but the more chaotic the budgies' unrehearsed antics became, the more the audience seemed to love it. Later in the show another waterproof cloth had to be quickly unrolled to fill the ring for the clowns to do their custard-pie act (or "slosh" routine, as it was professionally known). And so it went on.

The grand finale was a very impressive Hungarian illusionist called "Zelka". Normally illusionists perform their act on a stage with the audience facing them from just one direction. Consequently, most illusions are not "angle-proof" and cannot be viewed from the side, let alone from behind. But Zelka's act was done in the middle of the circus ring, with the audience completely surrounding him. His first trick was to raise a trapeze high up above the circus ring, and, once aloft, a small curtain dropped from a hoop above the trapeze. After a drum-roll from the band the curtain fell to the ground revealing his lovely female assistant sitting on the trapeze. Where on earth had she come from? I soon was to find out.

Zelka seemed a very aloof person, presumably because he spoke little English, and I never got to engage him in conversation although I really wanted to.

My week at the circus went all too quickly, but not only was it great fun, I had also learned quite a lot about the mysterious world of the sawdust ring, even though I had only just scratched the surface.

My time at the casino in the Tower Ballroom was fascinating. Although I have never been a gambler, the operational side of gambling is an intriguing business, and the manager showed me around and explained the workings of the different games. In one corner of the gaming floor was a small workshop where the "one-armed bandit" slot machines were repaired. I spent many an hour with the mechanic in there, learning the intricacies of these devices, most of which were entirely mechanical in their operation (with no electrical requirement other than to illuminate the colourful glass front) and used clockwork motors, and a mass of springs and levers inside, to separate the punters from their cash.

The card gaming tables were (and still are) a complete mystery to me, and the manager (whose name I'm afraid I've forgotten) realised that I had no aptitude in this direction. However, the Golden Nine roulette table was relatively simple and I spent several hours watching this being worked. The following day, when the casino was fairly quiet and before the evening crowds arrived, the manager asked if I'd like to have a go as a croupier and actually work the table. Hesitantly, I agreed. There were only a few punters, and for the next few hours, under the watchful eye of the experienced croupier, I helped a handful of happy holidaymakers lose some of their well-earned savings.

I cut short my time at the model village, when I found that my one and only job was to "mow" the grass of the miniature village green with a pair of scissors. So I moved on to help as a flyman at the show on the Wellington Pier. It was daunting to see massive great 20-stone men heaving on the ropes to raise and lower the scenery and curtains, and I, a scrawny 18-year old, was expected to help them. Fortunately, they made it clear that they would do the heaving, and I should "cleat-off" the rope around the large iron pegs to secure it.

The box office at the other pier just along the promenade was next. Mike and Bernie Winters were the stars of the show that year (if my memory serves me correctly) and the box office did a brisk trade from early morning to late evening. With no computers in those days, the pre-printed tickets were torn out of books representing the different seating blocks in the theatre. This was complicated by the fact that outside ticket agencies around the town also held tickets for sale, and during the afternoon of any given performance I had to cycle round Great Yarmouth and collect up any unsold tickets from the agencies, so that they could be sold at the main theatre box office.

I had already worked at the Windmill Theatre two summers previously, but had never been inducted into the mysteries of the finances of the operation. So for a few days (surprisingly, rather interesting days), I had explained to me the way payroll worked, box office receipts were accounted for, performing rights licenses negotiated and other financial matters.

At the Empire Cinema I found the same acne-ridden lad was in the projection room, but on this visit I was shown how the management booked the films through the London-based distributors, how the fire inspection licenses were obtained, how profits were made on icecream sales and so on.

The Aquarium Nightclub was next, and this necessitated a re-arrangement of my lodging hours with Miss Bond to allow me to rise at midday, and return after the club closed in the early hours of the morning. To my horror, I was told that I would be spending my time mainly "on the door". This meant standing, trembling, behind even larger bouncers than the flymen at the Wellington Pier, whilst they ejected drunks and troublemakers. After a few nights I plucked up the courage to stop trembling, but I still made sure I stood safely behind them whilst they wrestled with the clients.

But it was the Pleasure Beach that I found most fascinating. This was owned by a very larger-than-life gentleman called Albert Botton, who was a very good friend of Jack Jay's. His wife, Lottie, took me under her wing and undertook the task of introducing me to the wonders of the amusement park operation. I sat with her in the paybox of the Dodgems, I learned to "ride" the Waltzer and spin the cars, and, although I was never allowed to actually operate the brake on the Scenic Railway train, I sat behind the brakeman for 57 consecutive rides to observe his technique.

I was told to get to the park early the next morning to "walk the scenic track". This involved walking very slowly and with great concentration around the entire course of the giant wooden rollercoaster track looking for loose screws, damaged wood or any other form of potential safety hazard. It was blowing a gale straight off the North Sea as we got to the top of the high lift hill, and in those days safety harnesses and other health & safety protection were unknown. But I felt extraordinarily secure on top of this grand old structure. As we walked the track, I made a mental note of the way the whole thing worked. It faithfully obeyed Newton's Laws of Motion (physics "A" level had taught me that) but it turned the boring topic of conservation of potential and kinetic energy into a device of such thrills and fun. "Perhaps one day I might design and build one of these?" I thought.

In between all these fascinating glimpses of the other branches of showbusiness in that thriving seaside town, I had another role; that of assistant to Mr. Jay in his capacity of Chief Barker of the Variety Club. He managed his operations in such a way that he had loyal and very capable management at each of his various operations around East Anglia, and consequently he could devote a large amount of time to organizing the numerous charity fund-raising events during the summer season. But he needed a gofer to do some of the donkey-work, and that's where I fitted in. It went from the mundane and humble (more flyposting!) to the glamorous ("Pick up Morecambe and Wise from the

Carlton Hotel and bring them to the Wellesley Recreation Ground for the 3 o'clock kick-off of the celebrity football match" … "But Mr. Jay, I haven't got a car." … "Well take the Bentley then".

It was quite extraordinary how the big stars of the day with whom I had to meet behaved in such a pleasant and respectful manner to me as soon as they realised that I was Jack Jay's representative. Ken Dodd, Hughie Green, Cilla Black (… I must stop namedropping) and a dozen more household names were all entrusted to me to get them from event to event. It taught me that the bigger the star, the nicer they were. There was a sort of unwritten arrangement that on alternate Sundays (when the stars were not performing in their own shows) the Blackpool stars would come to Yarmouth for charity events, and the following Sunday the Yarmouth stars would go to Blackpool.

The Variety Club's main fundraising efforts were directed towards providing Sunshine Mini Coaches for disabled children's organisations all over Britain. The final event of the year was when the coach which had been bought through that season's fundraising in Great Yarmouth would drive onto Yarmouth Racecourse in front of a huge assembled crowd of holidaymakers, local dignitaries and celebrities, and be officially handed over to the group of recipient children and their parents. But Mr. Jay and I had a little surprise up our sleeves! The coach entered the arena, but it was followed by two others. The generosity of the people, stars and holidaymakers in Great Yarmouth that year had raised enough funds to buy three Sunshine Mini Coaches.

Jack Jay's success had come through sheer hard work, determination and astute business acumen. But he was also deep down a very kind and loyal employer. As Dot Edwards, the Windmill's box office manageress, once told me: "You either work for Jack Jay for a week, or a lifetime. There's never an in-between".

I was the exception. I worked for two summer seasons as a young lad for Mr. Jay. But I did gain the experience of a lifetime.

One afternoon when I returned to my lodgings for tea, I found Miss Bond slightly red-eyed as if she had been crying. I asked her if something was the matter, and all she would say was, "Oh, she did look *bootiful*. They'd done her up lovely". And then she demurely smiled.

"Who's done who up lovely?" I asked.

"The man from the *foondrel* place. She looked so *bootiful* and peaceful," she replied.

The broad Norfolk accent in which Miss Bond spoke was getting the better of me.

"What's a *foondrel* place?" I asked.

She looked at me as if I was a complete idiot.

"You know. The undertakers, where they arrange the *foondrel* when you die."

I was starting to get the picture.

"Who has died?" I queried.

"I don't know who she was," came the reply. "I was in Dewhurst's the butchers in King Street, and the lady behind me in the queue said that her next-door-but-one neighbour had died and they'd laid the body out in the coffin in her front room for everyone to come and see. She said she was going round after she'd done her shopping, so I thought I'd go along too. Half the queue in the butchers came along as well. Oh, she did look *bootiful*."

Some ladies take tea together in the afternoon, some play bingo, but Miss Bond liked to go and look at dead bodies of complete strangers.

It was during this second season at the Windmill Theatre that I learned another very valuable lesson into the mysteries of showbusiness. The show that season was a farce starring the comedian Jack Douglas, called "Don't Tell the Wife" by Sam Cree. To be honest, it was a pretty dreadful play, with lots of cheap humour centering on marital infidelity, sexy au pair maids, men's trousers falling down, and ladies being caught in their underwear. But the Great Yarmouth audiences thought it was all hilarious.

Imagine you were in the audience one night. The husband on stage trips and lands on the lap of the au pair maid on the sofa. In walks the wife carrying a tray of tea, sees here husband apparently caught *in flagrante* with the maid, and drops the tea tray. But on this particular night something goes wrong. She too trips, and accidentally throws the tea all over the scenery. The cast look concerned as the wallpaper of the set is obviously ruined. Then one of the cast sees the funny side and starts to giggle. This spreads to others onstage. They become helpless with laughter and can't get their lines out. The audience finds the whole thing hysterically funny along with those onstage. Jack Douglas cannot contain himself and has to turn his back to the audience to try to compose himself. He is obviously shaking with uncontrollable laughter.

The audience feel they have witnessed a very special occasion, and will talk about it the following morning to their fellow holidaymakers over breakfast in their guest houses. " ….. well, it was hilarious. They accidentally spilled the tea all over the scenery, and, laugh, the actors got a fit of the giggles ….. They had to stop the show….. I thought the lady next to me was going to wet herself ….."

But all was not quite as it seemed.

The whole "accidental" episode was written into the script from the very beginning. Every move was rehearsed, every supposedly uncontrolled laugh and giggle was carefully timed. The scenery was built so that the wallpaper could be wiped-down and dried with a hair-dryer during the interval (that was my job!!). The whole thing was all part of the show. But the audiences never realised. Within a few performances of the opening night, the professional cast didn't find any of this even remotely amusing. In fact the reason Jack Douglas used to turn his back on the audience was to conceal this. He simply jiggled his shoulders up and down to give the appearance of laughter from behind.

And I learned a lot from this. Audiences can be manipulated even when they don't realise it. They may think they are getting a backstage glimpse of our world, but we have everything under control. That's showbusiness!

Chapter 6

THE CAREER BEGINS

The end of the summer season at Great Yarmouth also marked the end of my amateurish dabblings in the entertainment business. I was about to go to the London Academy of Music and Dramatic Art and study the serious professional business of Stage Management and Technical Theatre.

Tower House was a landmark building at the crossroads of Cromwell Road and Earls Court Road in West London. Anyone travelling into London from the west of England via the M4 had to pass its rather gloomy bulk. And it was home to LAMDA.

A motley group of 14 students gathered in the lofty ground floor room at the front of the building on our first morning. We were aged between 18 and 24, some had experience in the amateur theatre, some in the provincial repertory theatre, and some no experience at all but had managed to blag their way through the interview. But all of us had backstage stars in our eyes. For some, becoming an acting assistant stage manager (acting ASM) was a foothold on the ladder to becoming a fully-fledged actor, but for me there were no such aspirations.

Robert Stanton, the course administrator re-introduced himself to us, along with a group of other specialist tutors who would be teaching the various courses upon which we were about to embark. It was only at this point that I started to realise what a diverse range of skills a stage manager was expected to have. As well as the obvious – cueing a show, stage lighting design, sound effects, scenery design and construction etc. – there was an extraordinary list of other quite exciting and daunting diverse topics in the syllabus – stage fighting and tumbling, dance and choreography, make-up, costume, voice production, music theory, play study, improvisation … the list went on and on.

Over the next few terms we would have to develop these skills in order to survive in the over-populated jungle of the live professional theatre.

We would quickly learn that the stage management hierarchy backstage is as follows:

The assistant stage manager (ASM) is the lowest of the low. Essentially, their job is to make the tea and to be generally abused by everybody else in the theatre. In theory, their responsibility is for the props – acquiring them during the rehearsal period, and setting them in place onstage (or on the actors' persons in the dressing rooms). An acting ASM also takes minor roles in the play (perhaps as a butler, or maid, or dead body). During the rehearsal period the ASM marks up the rehearsal room floor with coloured adhesive tape representing a fullsize plan of the eventual stage set, to enable the actors to move around the rehearsal space aware of the final location of doors, walls etc.

The deputy stage manager (DSM) is in charge of the Prompt Script (otherwise known as "The Book"). This is a copy of the script, interleaved with pages of plain paper. During the rehearsal period, everything that the actors do is written in this book next to the relevant line in the script. Every movement an actor makes onstage and every nuance is recorded in minute detail. Every cue that is about to happen offstage such as sound effects, lighting changes, and actors' impending entrances, is noted. In theory, by the time the rehearsal period ends, The Book contains a faithful record of what should happen in the future performances. Using this, the DSM marks up this book with technical cues in advance of each event, for example giving lighting or sound operators "Standby" cues with enough time to prepare for the event, and then "Go" cues at the precise moment the event has to happen. It is essentially a complete manual of the whole production, and by the time the show reaches the theatre, then in theory if all the cast were to die in a plane crash together with the director, the stage management would be able to rehearse a new cast and crew using The Book, and get the show on the road exactly as the director had intended.

During a performance, the DSM sits in the prompt corner at one side of the stage and "runs" the show, (rather like a conductor conducting an orchestra) using intercoms and signal cue lights to convey instructions to the various personnel around the theatre, and prompting the actors if they forget their lines. From 35 minutes before the curtain goes up (known in the theatre as "The Half") till the final curtain call at the end of the performance, the DSM is in control.

The stage manager (SM) is rather grand, and tends to be on Christian name terms with even the actors. He or she is responsible for keeping everything together, making sure that the cast have the right brand of gin in their dressing rooms, and walking around backstage looking very important in a formal tuxedo (if male) or twin-set and pearls (if female). Sometimes the SM also acts as production manager, and is responsible for paying the cast (if the theatre is lucky enough to have any money to do this) and fending-off creditor suppliers.

You will probably deduce from the tone of the three preceding paragraphs that I never climbed sufficiently high up the stage management ladder to become an SM.

The dynamics of our group of students were such that we naturally fell into several little cliques. Some were obviously actors-in-the-making. Others were techno-geeks who were fascinated by the intricacies of lighting and sound equipment ("Damian, pass me that Pattern 476 fresnel lens lantern with a sunrise gobo and a 48mm hook clamp" : "You what?"). And others were using the course as a stepping-stone to television studio management or other career paths within the entertainment profession. I drifted happily around from one clique to another, enjoying everything that LAMDA threw at me.

Most of the students were living in the vicinity of the college and its nearby theatre in Earls Court. But I was staying with my parents way out in the suburbs at the far end of the Piccadilly tube line. Three of the girls on the course, Vandra, Kate and Jenny, were renting a little mews flat just off Cromwell Road which was a stone's throw from the college, so many a late evening was spent there when I'd missed the last tube train home or was in need of some cheese on toast (only the Italians had heard of pizza at this time). One of these girls would become the most important person in my life when I married her many years later. But that's another story.

By the third term, we were considered sufficiently knowledgeable to be allowed out on tour with a group of actors from the second-year acting course. I was assigned the job of lighting a production of "Hobson's Choice", the classic play by Harold Brighouse. It was to tour for two weeks doing one-night-stands at various theatres, arts centres, village halls, and drab assembly rooms in provincial towns around the West Country. The small company of six actors and four stage management students were expected to muck-in and help each other. We toured around in a converted (and very dilapidated) old bus, which had most of the seats removed so that it could contain the entire show – scenery, costumes, props, lighting equipment, actors, and crew. It broke down on the outward journey 200 yards west of the Hogarth Roundabout (just six miles from our starting point) and continued to do so at similar intervals throughout the tour.

Our accommodation on tour was to be provided by local arts enthusiasts, and without exception I was kept well-fed and comfortable throughout. It was quite grueling. Every morning we would try to persuade the old bus to get us to the next venue. On arrival we would unload, and I would rig the lighting as best I could, according to whatever facilities the theatre had available. Other members of the cast and crew would erect the set and move into the dressing rooms, and by late afternoon we would be ready for a technical dress rehearsal. It was a complicated show with two sets, and a trapdoor in the stage (which we built as an extension in front of the theatre's own stage) and lots of intricate lighting and sound effects cues. After the show, we would strike the set, load everything into the bus, and be allocated a host family for the night (who would expect us to charismatically entertain them over dinner with witty tales of our glamorous theatrical lives).

And so it went on, night after night. Poole, Swanage, Dorchester, Exeter, Plymouth, Falmouth, Truro ..... they came and went. I would have hoped I could indeed relate to you some witty tales of misadventures of that tour, but, to be perfectly honest, I can't remember a thing other than that we got the curtain up every night on time, and the coach finally packed up at Swindon on the way back to London, never to be revived. (Rumour has it that an old derelict bus is still to be seen rusting away in a layby near Wootton Bassett, full of scenery, costumes props, and the dead body of a driver whose ghost still ...no, I'm being theatrical myself now. Forget it.). The tour was considered a big success, and was used by our tutors as a way of assessing our progress at the end of the course.

The final term in the second year was regarded as work experience, where the college found you a job, you got paid no wages whatsoever, but you still had to pay the college fees. This seemed very unfair, so I decided I would use my own initiative to find a job myself.

By this time, my parents had moved the family home to Wokingham in Berkshire. The nearest theatre to this was the Theatre Royal in Windsor. This classic playhouse theatre had recently been restored to its former velvety, goldy, crystal-chandeliery plushness, and had a fine reputation for its three-weekly rep (in other words, the shows ran for three weeks and then evaporated). I knew that I would have to write application letters to dozens of theatres for a job before I got even an interview, but I had to start somewhere. So a letter and my CV was duly sent to Windsor's Theatre Royal.

Two days after I posted the letter, my mother said when I'd got home from a hard day at the pub "Someone called Cyril phoned you, and left a number. I said you'd phone him back when you got in." Cyril? I knew no Cyril. I looked at the number he'd left and didn't recognise it. I dialed the number.

"Theatre Royal Windsor" announced the telephonist who answered the phone at the other end.

"Can I speak to Cyril please," said I, with an element of surprise in my voice.

"Cyril Gates? Our Production Manager?" queried the voice (who I later discovered was a lovely seductive middle-aged lady called Pauline, who chain-smoked and helped the actors empty their gin bottles in the dressing rooms).

"Yes, I think so."

And I was put through to Cyril Gates. I could tell immediately from his voice that here was a really fun guy with a wicked sense of humour, and a love for the theatre.

"Hello, John. I've got your letter. You have an rather interesting CV. Can we meet for a chat and a beer?"

So much for formal interviews. Here was a senior person in the management of one of Britain's most respected provincial repertory theatres talking to me like an old mate.

"Name the time and place!" I said.

"Thursday, 12:30 in the William the Fourth in Thames Street. OK?"

"OK!"

As soon as I walked into the pub I knew which of the customers was Cyril Gates. He was the slightly plump guy with the face of an aging cherub and twinkling mischievous eyes sat in the corner. When you get to know someone really well, you can strip down your conversation to the bare bones, so that whole sentences can be condensed into to single words. Somehow, this happened to us immediately.

"Pint?"

"Thanks"

"Bitter?"

"Guinness"

"Cheers!"

"Cheers!"

In order for the conversation to proceed it had to get a little more verbose. Cyril went through my CV and was particularly interested to hear what LAMDA was teaching its stage management students. He fired questions at me to test my knowledge. "How many minutes before curtain-up do you give the 15-minute call?" (No, the answer's not 15 minutes. I'll let you find out for yourself what it is). "How would you address an actor called John Smith over a tannoy or intercom?" (You always, ALWAYS, would say "Mr. Smith" and never use the Christian name, even if he was your brother). "Where do you take the prompt script after a performance ends?" (The answer is, you don't. It always must stay in the prompt corner, locked in a cupboard.)

I broke this last golden rule once the following year when I took a prompt script home after the show one night to make some amendments to it, and my car broke down the next day on the way back to the theatre. I had to cue a complete matinee performance of "The Importance of Being Ernest" from a public telephone box in Winkfield 10 miles from the theatre.

The conversation with Cyril Gates in the pub continued.

"Another pint Cyril?"

"Thanks"

"Bitter?"

"Yes."

"Cheers!"

"Cheers!"

And so it went on for nearly two hours. After the theory test, we moved onto the practical, where he asked about my unconventional and varied experiences during my two summer seasons in Great Yarmouth. Raunchy tales emerged (which I have no intention of recounting in this book, since I am writing this sober, unlike the slightly inebriated state I was in whilst chatting with Cyril Gates).

"Would it be possible to take a look around the theatre?" I asked.

"Sure" was the reply, and we walked across the road to the stage door. Whereas the Golders Green Hippodrome had a miserable old git as the stage doorkeeper all those years back, Windsor had ... Pauline. Cheery, helpful, attentive Pauline. That voice on the end of the phone. I was introduced to her, and two things emerged from her rouged lips ... a) "Lovely to meet you darling" and, b) a thick cloud of cigarette smoke.

We went through the heavy soundproofed door onto the stage. It wasn't huge by West End standards, but it was well-equipped with full counterweight flying, lofty flytower, and spacious wings. From the stage, the auditorium looked gorgeous. Then we went upstairs past the tiers of dressing rooms to Cyril's office at the very top of the building.

"We have a vacancy for an ASM. A production of a brand-new play by Terence Feely called "Who Killed Santa Claus?" starring Honor Blackman is starting rehearsal here on Monday, and one of our ASM's has left. Are you interested?"

Cyril went on to explain that they had two completely separate teams of stage management. One team would rehearse a show for three weeks during the daytime, whilst the other team was performing their show in the evening. Then you went into the theatre and performed your show for three weeks, whilst the other team rehearsed the next show in the daytime, and so on.

We discussed the delicate matter of money. I knew that ASM's were badly paid, but didn't realise just how badly! If I told you the weekly wage I agreed to, the sum would be so small on this page you would need a magnifying glass to read it.

So, on the following Monday, a nervous new ASM arrived at Pauline's stage door. She introduced me to Nick Prosser, my DSM (in other words, my immediate boss) and his easy-going friendly manner told me that we would get on well. The stage had been stripped of all the scenery for that evening's show – The Entertainer by John Osborne (and guess where the scenery went? … Up! Into the flies!) and the company of actors, who were all new to each other, were nervously introducing themselves to each other in the stalls. The director of the play, Anthony Wiles, made himself known to us. I thought that all we were waiting for now was the star of the show, Honor Blackman, to sweep-in in a theatrical manner.

Honor Blackman had been a film and television actress for many years, but it was her role as Cathy Gale in the hit TV series "The Avengers" that really brought her to the attention of the public, and then as Pussy Galore in the James Bond movie "Goldfinger" came international stardom. I was expecting a grand arrival. Then I realised she was already here. Quietly chatting away to everyone in the stalls. She walked up to me. ME! "You must be John, our ASM. I'm Honor. We're all going to have a lot of fun doing this, aren't we." Then she moved on to Nick.

And it was a lot of fun. The play was a whodunnit' with a very clever plot, and a twist at the end. Rehearsals went well, I obtained all the necessary props for the show, learnt all the tasks I had to undertake during the performance, and the opening night was well-received.

Roughly a week into the run, I was standing in the wings watching Honor Blackman onstage. It was that part of the plot in the play where critical things happened. Honor's character was alone onstage, and had to walk towards a chest of drawers and pull out a gun. She then had to cross to the other side of the stage and go to another piece of furniture, open another drawer, pull out a box of bullets, and load the gun with three bullets. Just before all this was about to happen, I was leaning against the rear of the proscenium arch behind the scenery, when I felt in my pocket. Oh no! The bullets were still in my pocket! I had forgotten to put them back in the drawer after the previous night's performance. Miss

Blackman was about to discover that the drawer was empty, and the whole plot would fall apart.

I watched in horror as she picked up the gun, crossed the stage, and opened the drawer.

Then something extraordinary happened.

Just as the script demanded, she took out the bullets and loaded the gun. It was impossible! There were no bullets in the drawer … they were still in my pocket. Then I realised what had happened. Without batting an eyelid, on realizing the drawer was empty Miss Blackman had mimed the whole thing. Her amazing professionalism had convinced, not only the audience, but also me, that she had loaded the gun with the bullets.

I was mortified. I was sure she would kill me. When the curtain came down, with great trepidation I knocked on her dressing room door.

"Come in"

"Miss Blackman, I'm so dreadfully sorry. I forgot to …"

"Since when did you start calling me "Miss" Blackman?" she interrupted me with a smile. "You call me Honor. And we all make mistakes, John. If that's the worst bollock you drop on this show, I, for one, will be a very happy actress." And she gave me hug.

As I said, the bigger the star, the nicer they are.

The next show was the Theatre Royal's Christmas Pantomime – "Babes in the Wood". This broke the routine cycle of three weeks rehearsal, three weeks run. For the pantomime, both stage management teams came together, and had a five week rehearsal and a six week run.

I was summoned to Cyril Gates' office. "John," he said with a serious expression on his face, "it is the tradition of this theatre that the ASM is given the honour of playing the pantomime horse in our Christmas pantomimes".

"Front or back?" I said.

"Front" came the reply. "Can you dance?".

"No" I assertively added.

"Tough, you're going to have to learn. You get an extra £6 a week on top of your stage management wages."

And that was the end of the matter.

My first task was to find the wretched costume in the wardrobe store, de-bug it and dry off the mildew, then set about renovating the intricate mechanism in the head that made it do all the usual daft things like wiggle its ears, roll its eyes, wink, as well as open and close its mouth. These mechanical features were operated by strings that hung down from inside the head into the body, so you could pull on the strings in front of you and, hopefully, reduce the audience to tears of laughter. I took the head apart, to give it a thorough service. I then added a surprise new feature that nobody would know about until the opening night; I would make it cry. Not just little teardrops, but powerful jets of water that would blast out from the corners of the eyes, across the stage, and into the audience. But that was my little secret.

Then the whole thing was carted-off to the wardrobe department to be dry cleaned and smartened-up.

"I can't dance, Nick" I said to my DSM.

"They say Julie Dinton is going to be your back-half" Nick replied, "and she's a dancer. She'll teach you." As it turned out, Julie taught me a lot. And they say that Millie the Filly's soft shoe shuffle is still talked about in the stables of pantomime horses to this day.

Another summons to Cyril Gates' office. "Do you know anything about dry ice?"

"DO I KNOW ANYTHING ABOUT DRY ICE!!!!! I'm an expert". Well, I thought I was an expert, but as it turned out dropping pieces of dry ice into a bucket of hot water at the school production of Midsummer Night's Dream to produce the carpet of low-lying mist so characteristic of ballet dream sequences was insufficient to fill the large stage of the Theatre Royal, Windsor. It transpired that a company on an old airfield in nearby Maidenhead called Concept Engineering manufactured smoke machines, dry ice machines, cobweb guns and all manner of special effects equipment for the entertainment industry. I paid them a visit, specifically for the purpose of finding out how their machines worked, and making a copy myself.

Essentially, a dry ice fog machine consists of an electrically-heated boiler full of hot water into which a basket of crushed solid carbon dioxide (dry ice) can be lowered, and the resulting heavy white vapour is blown out of the front of the machine by a powerful fan. What could be easier to make? So I enlisted the help of Norman the theatre's stage carpenter, bought a secondhand Burco water boiler, fitted a Vent Axia extractor fan in the top ….. et voila!

Now, dry ice is complicated and expensive to obtain. It has to be delivered daily, as it melts in no time, so we arranged the first delivery to take place on the day of the dress rehearsal, with no opportunity to test the machine's efficacy beforehand. The Babes in the Wood were lost. The woodland glade was filled with fairies to protect them from the wild creatures of the forest, and according to the script, a gentle mist drifted around the magical forest floor. What actually happened was that when the basket of dry ice was lowered into the tank of boiling water, it erupted into a writhing mass of steam, the machine shook violently, I rammed on the lid, and started the fans. A huge wall of dense fog rolled onto the stage, completely submerging the fairies, rolled down the stage, across the footlights and into the orchestra pit. "How the f@©k are we expected to play the music when we can't even see the f@©king instruments!" exclaimed the trombonist.

Fortunately, the director, producer and choreographer watching the rehearsal from the stalls saw the funny side of things, and called out "A little less dry ice in future please, John".

I had still not revealed my secret addition to Milly the Filly's repertoire of novelty features. On the opening night, when Nurse Dahlia (the pantomime dame, played by a lovely guy called Barrie Gosney) and Milly are searching for the Babes, they are very sad. Time to try out my new surprise. I squeezed the bulb that pressurized the water container, the pipe burst and deposited the entire tank of water down inside my trouser leg. It was very obvious to the audience that whoever was inside the costume had a serious incontinence problem, and wherever we went on stage we left a trail of embarrassing liquid on which everyone slipped and skidded.

One of the scenes involved a custard pie routine between Nurse Dahlia and Rascally Richard (played by Douglas Ridley) when they were supposedly cooking pies in the castle kitchens. Neither of them had done this sort of work before, and had no idea what the pies (or, slosh) should be made of. It was down to me to get this sorted. I cast my mind back to the time when I was ringboy at the circus in Great Yarmouth and wracked my brains as to what the clowns made their slosh from. They were very secretive about this. I could distinctly remember it had to be whipped-up just before they went on, or the gooey foam would collapse in a wet mess. And they were using cans of powder, and written on the labels was the name ... oh, what was that name ... SHAVALLO. That was it. Shavallo! It was a professional powdered shaving soap made specifically for barbers.

I found an old traditional barbershop in Windsor. It looked as if it was something straight out of a Dickens novel. "Have you heard of something called Shavallo?" I asked the ancient proprietor, hoping he would be able to answer before he passed peacefully away to that Great Salon in the Sky. "Yes, but they stopped making it a couple of years back. But," he replied, "I think my wholesaler still has a few cans though." He gave me the name of a barbers' wholesaler in Slough, and off I went. "Have you got any cans of Shavallo" I asked. "Yes, how many do you want?" "I'll take the lot! Every can you've got."

I came out with 150 cans of this precious and obsolete product, which I paid for out of my own money. I sold 20 cans to the Theatre Royal for the pantomime, and kept the remaining 130 cans for myself. And for the next few years I had a nice little sideline selling my own stage custard pie mix in sachets, which I called "Gundge", to theatres and circuses around the country, improving the formula by adding colouring and a foam stabilizer (actually, cellulose wallpaper paste). "Just add water and whisk, for a long-lasting slosh foam" ran my advert in "The Stage" newspaper.

After the pantomime season ended, it was back to the regular three-weekly schedule. For one production I was looking for a particular type of old-fashioned gas streetlamp to embellish a scene, and was told that they had a very good range of all types of streetlamps in the property department at Pinewood Studios. Since Pinewood was only just down the road from Windsor, I made an appointment to see the head of the prop department there, Arthur Franks. At this time (in the early '70s), Pinewood was churning out James Bond films at the rate of almost one every 18 months, and Bray Studios not far away was producing Hammer

Horror films three times as rapidly. Then there was Shepperton Studios a few miles in the other direction. So Windsor was slap-bang in the middle of the greatest concentration of major film studios in Europe.

I met Arthur, who was very helpful and he showed me round the cavernous prop department, which seemed to contain virtually every conceivable piece of embellishment any stage, TV or film set could require. I discussed the charge for hiring the streetlamp and arranged for a van to collect it the next day.

On my way out of the building I bumped into a gentleman whom I'd seen at Concept Engineering a few months earlier when I was on my fog machine spying mission. His name was Mike Hope. It turned out that he owned the company, together with another associate company called I.E.S. Projects. He explained that although Concept produced the range of standard special effects products, his other company I.E.S. made one-off special effects for big films, and they were currently working on the James Bond film which was in production at that time at Pinewood "Diamonds Are Forever".

He said that, if he'd remembered correctly, he didn't think that I had actually bought or hired a dry ice machine from him for the Theatre Royal's pantomime after my visit. I cheekily admitted to him that the only purpose of my visit to his factory was to see how they worked so I could make one myself. "Did you?" he asked. "Yes" I said. "And did it work?" "Rather too well!" I replied. He smiled in a good-natured way.

As we parted to go our separate ways, he jokingly said "Call me if you ever want a job!" and handed me his card.

That card proved rather useful.

Chapter 7

THE MAGIC BOND

During the rehearsal period for one production at the Theatre Royal, Windsor, I had had to obtain as a stage prop a full-size human skeleton to decorate the stage set. On approaching the normal stage property hire company we used, I was told that the cost would be over £100 a week to hire, including a special insurance premium due to the value and fragility of the thing. I said that was ridiculous as I only wanted a dummy skeleton which would look realistic from a distance. I was told that they only had expensive medical replicas which were perfect in every anatomical detail. So I had to settle for that. It occurred to me that there had to be a market for a fairly durable, dummy human skeleton for stage use which was more realistic than the cheap ones found in joke shops, but not as perfect as the expensive medical replicas.

I decided I would find a way to cast an entire skeleton in rubber latex using plaster piece-moulds. I learned the technique of how to do this by trial and error, and located a supplier of rubber latex casting compound. But first, I needed a <u>real</u> human skeleton from which to make the moulds.

Some months previously I had sold some of my Gundge custard pie powder to an extraordinary guy called Danny Lynch. He prided himself on being able to get anything for anybody. His house was brimming full of bizarre curios from shrunken heads to a model replica of the Taj Mahal made entirely out of toothpicks. I'd set him the challenge of finding me a human skeleton.

It turned out to be not much of a challenge at all, as he had located one within a matter of a few hours at a very good price (although, not being too familiar with the market in human skeletons, I wasn't too sure what the going rate was!). The deal was done, and the thing duly arrived in a wooden box complete with a crumbling certificate of provenance proving that it hadn't just been robbed from a grave, but was from a medical supply company called Adam Rouilly in 1927, who had imported it from a firm called Reknas in Calcutta. (I have since discovered that the Adam Rouilly company is still in existence to this day, and sells the very replica plastic medical skeletons I had rejected).

On laying out the collection of bones, I discovered to my alarm that the "very good price" was due to the fact that the skeleton did not belong to any one person, but was made up of an assortment of bones from a number of different-sized individuals. I had to set-to with saw and plaster and remake the bones into a symmetrical set. It was a most gruesome job.

The plaster piece moulds were then made from these bones, which was a very complicated and lengthy task. The skull mould, for example, was made up of five separate parts which fitted together like a three-dimensional jigsaw puzzle. The moulds were filled with latex rubber casting compound, and left to "gel" for ten minutes. During this period the latex solution formed a skin where it was in contact with the absorbent plaster, so that when the liquid was emptied from the mould it left behind a rubber coating which cured into a flexible rubber material.

On opening the moulds 12 hours later the castings could be removed and trimmed of their spurious parts. The rubber limb bones were threaded together using nylon chord, and then assembled onto a wooden framework which supported the chest, spine, pelvis, shoulder blades and skull.

In this way I was able to mass produce a very realistic dummy skeleton which I sold to stage property hire companies. Then it occurred to me that fairground Ghost Train operators might find them useful, so I put an advert in the weekly newspaper of the travelling showmen, "The World's Fair", and orders started flooding in.

My wages in stage management were pitifully low, and although I loved the work and people, it became apparent to me that I was earning far more from my sidelines than the official fulltime work at the theatre. Only when we were performing a show in the evening did I have the daytime free to engage in my own enterprises, so, reluctantly, I took the big step of handing in my notice at the Theatre Royal Windsor. Cyril Gates received it with his usual good grace, and said that if the theatre needed any special props or effects made he'd be in touch. In fact, a few months later he asked me to build a crazy comedy car for the next pantomime, which I duly did.

After the pantomime had finished its run, Cyril asked me if I knew of anybody who might be interested in buying the car. Purely on spec, I made him an offer and bought it back from him myself. I rented a garage next to my workshop at the rear of Sindlesham Village Stores and overhauled the car and its many novelty features. One of my "Gundge Custard Pie Mix" circus customers happened to phone me up to order some more sachets of this unique product (!) and I asked him if he knew anybody who wanted to buy a crazy circus clown's comedy car. He asked me to send him some photos and details, and within a week I had done a deal.

The purchaser was Stromboli the fire eater and sword swallower. With his wife Sylvia, the act of "Stromboli and Sylvia" was extremely successful in the clubs of the northwest of England. But he felt that an untapped outlet for his skills was playing the open-air arenas, carnivals, and galas in the summer. The act was very visual, and the sight of him blowing huge balls of fire across carnival fields was appealing to agents and bookers. But he had the problem of how to get his various props and apparatus into the ring, and this is where the idea of driving the crazy car with his entire act onboard could be a solution. And as part of his new routine, he could then drive the car around the perimeter of the arena and make the doors fall off, the radiator explode, the back seat collapse, and so on.

So it was arranged that I'd deliver it to him at his home in Astley just outside Manchester. I hired a van, and got two steel ramps organised so that I could wheel the car in and out. Very early one morning I set off for the long journey up north. There were very few motorways then, and so the route took me through the pretty villages of the Cotswolds. It was about 6 o'clock in the morning when I found myself driving through the quaint village of Chipping Campden, so I decided to take a break for a drink of coffee from my thermos flask. I parked the van outside the village Post Office.

Within a few minutes various other vehicles were arriving and parking either side of me. They were the postmen turning up for their shift, and were waiting for the head postmaster to arrive and unlock the sorting office door. It was a warm morning, and we all had our vehicle windows down, so in no time at all friendly conversation had started.

"Where are you heading?" asked one of the waiting postmen. I answered.

"What have you got in your van?" asked another. I answered.

"You've got a WHAT? I've got to see this!".

He jumped out of his vehicle and looked in through the rear windows of the van. "Hey, lads, you'll never believe what this guy has got inside his van!" he shouted to his colleagues. In no time at all, they'd all crowded round my van, and had opened the back door.

"Can we have a better look?" said one.

So I got the two steel ramps out, and drove the comedy car down onto the road. Obviously a demonstration was called for.

I drove up the High Street with a postman in the passenger seat next to me, and two more in the rear seat behind. Outside the knitting shop I made one of the doors fall off. Opposite the Noel Arms Hotel the radiator exploded in a cloud of steam. Just past the Bantam Tea Rooms a tyre inner-tube blew out (actually a pink balloon concealed within the wheel arch). Finally outside Lloyds Bank the rear seat collapsed and tipped its two unsuspecting occupants onto the road behind.

Oh what fun we had!!!!!

The good people of Chipping Campden were still fast asleep tucked up in their beds. If only they could have seen what their postmen were getting up to along the road outside!

My journey up to Manchester continued, and a delighted Stromboli and Sylvia took delivery of their new crazy car, and have used it in their act for many years ever since.

Another area of work I developed was manufacturing illusions for professional magicians, using the knowledge I had obtained from my old Uncle Tommy many years before. These illusions would be built to order, to the specification of the client. On one occasion a well-known illusionist asked me to build a Sword Cabinet, a standard trick that is performed frequently by stage magicians. He gave me the dimensions he wanted in order for his female assistant to fit in it, and I commenced manufacture.

When performed, the effect the audience sees is as follows:- Onstage is a cabinet with a top-opening lid, just large enough for a young lady to squeeze inside in a crouching position. The box is mounted clear of the ground on a small table. Polished steel swords are thrust into the cabinet through slots in the two sides, and then, to complete the illusion, the front of the box is opened up to reveal that the girl has vanished, and the cabinet is just full of a mass of criss-crossed sword blades.

It's not particularly original or clever, so I'll explain how it's done. The tabletop on which the cabinet sits has a slight thickness to it (which forms a very shallow box about six-inches deep). This is concealed either by a short fringed tablecloth, or by beveling the edges to make the top appear much thinner than it actually is. When the girl gets into the box, she sits cross-legged in the base of the table top, so her legs are contained in this, and the rest of her body is in the main cabinet with her back up against the rear face of the box. The swords fill the space immediately in front of her, and a black roller blind is pulled down between her and the swords so that when the front of the box is opened, it appears as if she has vanished.

After I had completed construction of the illusion (and before I painted and finished it) I thought I'd see if I could get into the box myself. Not only did I slip into it with ease, I discovered that I was able to twist myself around so that I could get my entire body into the little table base, leaving the main cabinet genuinely empty.

This made me think!

I completed the illusion as instructed, and delivered it to a very satisfied customer. Then I set to work again, and built another box ..... this time without the roller blind, but with a second opening panel at the back. In this way, not only was the front of the box opened, but also the back, so that the audience could see right through this. The box really was empty!

Very occasionally I used to reluctantly resurrect my old act and perform it, so I added this new illusion that I had invented to the repertoire. My female assistant would appear to refuse to get into the box, so we would change places and she would perform the trick on me. I was of regular build, 5ft. 11ins tall, and when I climbed into the box it looked a real squeeze (or, at least, I made it look that way!). Normal audiences were not particularly impressed by this illusion any more than the others, but on one occasion we found ourselves performing in front of an audience composed entirely of magicians and their guests, as the cabaret at a regional magical society annual dinner.

When we started to perform the Stake Box (I had changed the swords to pointed wooden stakes, to make it a little different) the rather jaded audience sat back rather unimpressed. They had seen it done a hundred times before. In went the stakes. (Yawn!). The front of the box was opened. (More yawns!). But then the back of the box was opened. They could see all the way through. My assistant passed her arms through the box from back to front. The box really was empty!

Even I, tucked inside the base of the box, could hear a gasp from the audience. The magicians thought they knew how the trick was done, and most of them probably did, but they couldn't understand exactly how it was done. We got a standing ovation. The magical press (a weekly magazine called "Abra") picked it up. The illusion was the talk of the magical fraternity. We were asked to perform at magical conventions all over the country. People tried to copy it, but nobody ever found out how I was able to do it!!!

One day I had a phone call from a man named Bernard Hughes, who had seen me perform the Stake Box at a cabaret in the Café Royal in Regent Street, London. He and his father ran a company called the Hughes House of Magic, and they were one of the biggest suppliers of stage magic props and illusions in the world. He said he was impressed with the illusion, and asked if I would be interested in licensing him the rights to manufacture and sell it. I said that might be a problem, but I was happy to go and see him (mainly because I was fascinated to see his workshops and meet his father Jack Hughes, whose name was a legend in the magical fraternity).

I travelled up to Kings Lynn in Norfolk with the Stake Box in the back of my car. I arrived at The Grange, which was a huge rambling old rectory just outside the town, and the headquarters of the Hughes House of Magic. I rang the doorbell, and when I saw the person who answered it, my jaw dropped open in amazement.

"Zelka!" I gasped.

A huge grin appeared on Bernard Hughes' face. Yes, he was the mysterious and aloof Hungarian illusionist who spoke little English and whom I had seen performing while I was that apprentice ringboy at the Hippodrome Circus. But he was neither aloof nor Hungarian, and spoke perfect English (having been born in Cricklewood to English parents!) It reminded me of Uncle Tommy who had lived his professional life as Vadir the Russian acrobat.

The Grange was an intriguing place. It was both family home to Bernard and his very glamorous wife (and Zelka's assistant) Honor and his charming parents. It was also showroom and workshop for their magic supply business. I assembled the illusion in the only place I could find in the house that wasn't cluttered with stage props and magical equipment … at the foot of the huge oak staircase in the cavernous hall. I explained that I'd get into the box, and that Bernard should then push the wooden stakes through the holes in one side, and they would emerge from the other. Then he should open the front and back of the box, and have a good look inside. This he did. The whole family then peered in, and much head-scratching took place. They knew full-well where I was, but they couldn't figure out quite how I'd done it.

I got out, and allowed Honor to have a go. She'd been a "box jumper" (the crude term sometimes given to illusionists' assistants) ever since Bernard had plucked her out of a troupe of dancing girls many years before, but she wriggled and squeezed, and just couldn't manage to get in. Bernard and Jack decided that if they were to manufacture and sell the trick they would have to build the table base much bigger in order to sell it on the mass market, and I said I wasn't happy with this. So we all agreed that perhaps this wasn't the best illusion for them to add to their stock catalogue range.

I then pulled out of my pocket a small reel of Super-8 movie film. It was the old film I had shot as a child performing the Metamorphosis Substitution Trunk for Uncle Tommy, and I'd found it in the back of a drawer some months previously. The Hughes' didn't have a movie projector, but after some phoning around to local friends in Kings Lynn, one was found and the film loaded into it. I hadn't seen it for nearly twenty years. They all agreed that as a nine year old kid, I was quite adept at performing this. Hughes House of Magic manufactured a version of this trick, but far more professionally made than mine. They called it the Hat Box Substitution Trunk (as it was shaped like an octagonal hat box, which folded up very cleverly completely flat for travelling). The problem they had selling this illusion was that it couldn't be performed just from reading some written instructions, but needed considerable coaching and practice to learn how to do it slickly. Jack asked me if, whenever he sold a Hat Box, he could give the purchaser the option of a day's coaching from me (at extra cost) to teach them the trick. Over the next few years, quite a lot of customers took him up on this option, and I travelled around the country and met many lovely people in the process (some of whom are still my good friends to this day).

I returned from one such tutoring session with a rather hopeless but enthusiastic amateur magician in Bristol (his corpulent physique made him most unsuitable for squeezing into boxes, but his determination was admirable!), and I found myself passing the town of Maidenhead. This was where the engineering company who made the smoke machines and film special effects was based. The guy I'd met had given me his card. Now, what was his name? Mike Hope. That was it.

On the off-chance I called into the factory on a trading estate next to White Waltham Airfield. I was told that Mike was not in the office, but that if I left a phone number he would contact me. This he did the following day. I explained that I had met him at Pinewood Studios some months earlier (I don't think he remembered me) and he'd offered me a job. This came as something of a surprise to him, but we arranged a meeting at his office for a few days later.

Mike turned out to be a big man with a big personality and enormous courage. To survive in the terrifying world of feature film special effects you need to quote a fixed price for delivering an effect without having a clue how you are going to achieve it! It is all done on hunches, intuition and experience, and only after a contract has been signed do you start the process of devising how you are actually going to achieve what you have agreed to do. And invariably it has to be done on an incredibly short timescale. Contracts worth many tens of thousands of pounds had to be undertaken sometimes with less than a week's notice.

The main claim to fame of Mike's partner, Bill Nunn, was that he had invented The Long Egg Machine. Normally hard boiled eggs are, well, egg-shaped! But Bill's machine made one long, continuous hard-boiled egg. Why on earth would anyone want a long, continuous hard-boiled egg? You may well ask. Have you ever had a slice of rectangular ham-and-egg pie and wondered how every slice always has a perfect circle of hard-boiled egg in the middle, with a disc of yellow yolk surrounded by a ring of white? The answer is that the pie contains boiled egg produced by Bill's Long Egg Machine. Egg yolk is put in one hopper, and egg white is put in another, and out of the other end of the machine is extruded one long continuous hard-boiled egg. Bill deserves serious recognition for this life-saving gastronomic invention, and maybe a posthumous knighthood.

Mike must have identified that someone with my theatrical background could be a useful addition to his team of engineers, and he invited me to join. I was a member of the actor's union, Equity (through my stage management days at Windsor), which meant that whenever a special effect had to be operated by someone on-camera, I had the right union qualifications to do this. Although I was self-employed, I worked with Mike and his partner Bill Nunn for many years.

As well as film effects, we produced elaborate stage machinery for the Royal Opera House in Covent Garden, the Royal Shakespeare Company in Stratford-upon-Avon, and Sadler's Wells Opera at the London Coliseum. I helped them to extend the range of their standard products to include a battery-operated smoke machine, and a new type of artificial cobweb gun which fitted into the chuck of an ordinary electric drill. (Rubber solution was poured into the container, the drill switched on, and the effect was as if a million spiders had spun their webs all over everything. A light dusting of fuller's earth, and total decrepitude resulted!)

We also created special effects for big rock concerts. In those days there were no giant TV screens or lasers with which to produce spectacular moving images, so all the effects were done with lighting, pyrotechnics and huge mechanical devices. Perhaps the biggest and most incredible of all was the debut concert of Pink Floyd's album "Dark Side of the Moon" which took place at London's Earls Court arena in 1973. The scale of the spectacle was enormous, and included me being launched up high into the roof of the arena over the heads of the audience dressed as an astronaut, and a half-life size plane flown from the back of the auditorium onto the stage where it crashed in a ball of flames.

But it was the film effects that were the most fun, and the most memorable.

Now, before I go any further, you must understand two things. Firstly, that film special effects are created by a huge team of people, and that I was just one of their number. So if you see me using the word "I" in the next few paragraphs, instead in most cases you should read that as "we". I cannot take credit for these effects (nor can any other one individual). Secondly, although nowadays most large special effects are created digitally in post-production, in the mid-70's there was no such thing as computer-generated imaging, and everything had to be done for real. If you needed to blow up a castle, you really built a castle and blew it up. If you wanted a landslide (as we did in the film The Railway Children) you created a real, fullsize landslide. Although there was a huge amount of fakery going on, it was nevertheless real explosions, real fire, gigantic complicated machinery, and huge film sets. Boy, did we have fun!!!!

For example, in Ken Russell's film 'The Boyfriend', Twiggy and Christopher Gable are seen dancing on a giant revolving record on a huge antique gramophone. Whereas nowadays they would simply dance on a static green floor with a green background, and a digitally-created model of the gramophone would be super-imposed onto the shot afterwards, back then at Elstree Studios we built exactly what you saw ….. an enormous revolving turntable, with an inner centre representing the label which could revolve in the opposite direction, and the whole thing decorated to look like an old 78 gramophone. I was in charge of operating this colossal machine during filming.

You probably will not remember this, but on the old-fashioned gramophones, built into the deck was a small chrome-plated recessed dish where you could keep the spent needles. On our giant version, this was the size of a Jacuzzi. I was quietly minding my own business during a lunch break reclining comfortably in the bottom of the dish when someone slipped in beside me. It was Twiggy who asked me who I was and what I did. And I asked her about her life as one of the world's most famous fashion models. We spent a very happy 15 minutes putting the world to rights in that needle-dish.

Horror films were the most fun to work on. Invariably the atmosphere on a horror film set is anything but spooky, sinister or horrific. It tends to be very jolly, since the paraphernalia of film production takes away any strangeness. However, the old house next to Bray Studios, Oakley Court, was a Victorian Gothic mansion of terrifying appearance, and was deliberately kept in a state of semi-dereliction for use as a film set for Hammer Horror films. Since location film crews use their own generators for the electrical power for their lights, the mains power supply to the house had been permanently disconnected due to the dilapidated state of the building, and whenever we were doing any effects there we had to explore the spooky corridors by torchlight. (Oakley Court has since been renovated and turned into a very posh luxury hotel!)

We were filming 'The Rocky Horror Picture Show' at Oakley Court. If you have ever seen this film, the main character, Dr. Frank-N-Furter, (played by Tim Curry) makes his first appearance by slowly descending in an elevator whilst singing the number "Sweet Transvestite". Now, Oakley Court didn't have an elevator, and even if it had it would probably be as dilapidated and unsafe as the building around it, so we had to fake one up. We used a standard forklift truck, onto the forks of which a dummy lift cage was constructed, with a piece of scenery representing an ancient lift shaft wrapped around the whole thing.

The shot only involved seeing the lift descending from the ceiling, so the range of the big forklift truck was sufficient to produce the necessary movement. I was comfortably sat in the cab of the forklift, and simply operated the forks up and down according to the director's instructions. In the middle of shooting, suddenly the main electrical generator failed and all the lights went out. We were all plunged into pitch darkness. I had the presence of mind to turn on the forklift's headlights, and the scene I saw before me will be etched in my mind for ever. The entire cast and crew were huddled together in frozen postures of sheer terror. At last they felt some of the fear their future audiences would experience.

But it was the James Bond films that were the most amazing to work on. They had some of the largest budgets ever attributed to feature films of their time, and employed the best people in the business. And everything was based in Britain, using British talent. The huge '007 Stage' at Pinewood Studios (one of the biggest in the world) was built in 1976 specifically for 'The Spy Who Loved Me', and the size, scale and detail of the sets built for subsequent Bond movies on this massive stage had to be seen to be believed.

In 'Live and Let Die', James Bond visits the Fillet of Soul restaurant in New Orleans (owned by the movie's villain, Mr. Big) on several occasions, each time being detained by a different devious method. He decides that the one place in the restaurant where he will be safe from capture is immediately in front of the cabaret stage, in full view of all the other diners. There is no way he can be kidnapped from there. He seats himself at a table immediately in front of the singer onstage, and as she reaches the crescendo in the song, the whole table and chairs at which Bond is seated drop through the floor, the void being immediately filled by a sliding trapdoor, and waiters come on with a replacement set of furniture.

The scene was shot on the stage at Pinewood, and I was involved in constructing and operating the lift and trapdoor machinery. The director, Guy Hamilton, made it very plain that it all had to operate in an instant, at an alarming speed, so that as the floor began to drop, the replacement trapdoor had to simultaneously start its movement across the void, sliding in place towards James Bond just a hair's-breadth above his head. It was very scary sitting in the chair, seeing two tons of steel and wood whizzing straight towards your face. If the lift mechanism failed, the trapdoor would slice the top off your head, like a knife slicing the top off a boiled egg.

Guy told Roger Moore in no uncertain terms that he must not flinch at all as this was happening. He had to stay completely passive and calm, and not duck his head down as the floor passed over, or show any signs of alarm. Roger said that he would do it in one take, and only one take.

But first he wanted to see *me* do it that way!

I can now tell the world that I stood in for James Bond on that rehearsal shot. The cameras rolled, I took my place at the table, and – THUD – down went the floor. Heading straight for my face at a million miles an hour was the sliding trapdoor, I felt it brush my hair (and I did have hair in those days) as it whistled over my head as I continued my descent into the dark basement pit. And then – SLAM – it shut tight above me.

The crew applauded, Roger Moore shook my hand, and he took my place. And, needless to say, he did it absolutely perfectly in just one take. How cool is that!

But the special effect sequence in the film that everyone remembers was the bus chase. James Bond is escaping from the police in a beaten-up double-decker bus. He is driving along a narrow road with a police car in hot pursuit when he sees ahead of him a low bridge. He crashes into the bridge, the top deck of the bus is sheered off, and lands on top of the pursuing police car which then swerves around and crashes.

This was how we did it. Two identical old London Transport double-decker buses were purchased. One was sent straight to the props department at Pinewood to be made to look old and decrepit, whilst the other trundled over to our works on White Waltham Airfield. We removed the roof and superstructure of the top deck, and installed a sliding track on its floor, rather like a huge version of the smooth drawer runners you get in modern fitted kitchens. Onto this sliding mechanism a framework with a lightweight fibreglass replacement of the roof was built. Where the front of the bus hit the bridge, six replacement thin aluminium shells were made that would crumple on impact. In this way, the crash could be repeated up to six times for six takes.

The sliding top deck was then spring-loaded with giant bungee chords, so that it would be fired with enormous force off the back of the bus. It was held in place by explosive links, which were detonated by electronic impact sensors fixed to the inside of the aluminium shells.

A totally separate rig consisting of a very lightweight facsimile of the top deck was suspended from the jib of a crane, and dropped onto the police car as a separate shot. And a third rig fitted over the police car, so it could drive along the road and appear to swerve. I am pleased to say that three of the replacement aluminium crumple shells were never used.

The next Bond film was 'The Man with the Golden Gun' for which I was involved in the construction of the solar-powered laser gun that Scaramanga intends to use to conquer the world. It consisted of a fibreglass housing suspended from an aluminium column on which it articulated. The barrel of the gun was a perspex tube, up the centre of which was fitted a red neon tube to simulate the laser beam.

The laser gun in my workshop

During filming, the art director, a great guy with a wicked sense of humour called John Graysmark, took me to one side and said was there any way I could make the barrel glow in an ominous way just before the beam actually fired. I lashed up a blue light inside the gun, and tried it but it didn't really have any effect. But then I had a flash of inspiration. I found an old piece of rubber tubing on the set, drilled a hole in the housing of the gun and threaded the tubing through into the perspex barrel. By blowing cigarette smoke through the rubber tube into the gun, the inside of the barrel glowed an ominous high-tech blue. So whenever you see the film, think of me lying on the floor under the gun just out of camera range, with a packet of Rothmans in my pocket, puffing away up the rubber tube.

But it was another sequence in this film that marked a significant turning point in my career … The Funhouse.

Chapter 8

THE FUN BEGINS

The last effect that I worked on in 'The Man with the Golden Gun' was in the Funhouse scene.

The movie's deranged villain, Scaramanga, played by Christopher Lee (who in real life was the nicest, least-threatening person you could wish to meet), had built his own fairground funhouse in his palatial lair. James Bond is lured into this, and experiences its many diabolical delights. One of which was a staircase, the treads of which could all tilt so as to form a smooth and slippery surface. I was involved in designing and constructing this.

But whilst we were filming this, there was one thing which seemed to be missing all the time ... the sound of real people laughing and screaming and having fun. That's what a Funhouse was all about, and ours was eerily quiet.

All the time I was working in the film industry, I really missed the live audience. From my early years, the sound of people being entertained was magic to my ears. In film production you are totally isolated from the very people you are striving to amuse, thrill, shock or amaze. It seemed such a shame that what we were doing had to be filmed, dubbed, edited, and eventually after many months of post-production would be projected onto a screen in a cinema. Yet whenever we had any VIP's or other visitors come onto the film sets and saw what we were doing, they really were amused, thrilled, shocked or amazed. If only there was some way we could bring a _live_ audience to see what we were achieving. And then I thought about the concept that was starting to proliferate in America ... the Theme Park.

That's exactly what was needed in Britain, combining the techniques of the movie industry (scenery and special effects) with the machinery of the amusement park (rides etc.) to entertain a live audience. A number of big companies had looked into doing this, but had gone in with enormous grandiose schemes that never got off the ground. A more subtle lower-key approach might work. But how could I do it? I needed to know more about the amusement industry than my short time at the Pleasure Beach in Great Yarmouth had allowed.

Even when I was working on major film productions, I still kept making and selling my dummy human skeletons. I advertised these in the newspaper of the fairground trade, The World's Fair, and whenever I had a few hours to spare (or en-route to a film location) I'd bung a few skeletons in the boot of my car and find the nearest travelling fair to peddle my wares to showmen with ghost trains and haunted houses.

My delivery of skeletons to the fairgrounds would cause quite a stir. I used to wrap them in clear plastic bags, so that when I walked onto a "gaff" (the colloquial term for a travelling fair) carrying my wares, they were plain for all to see.

On one occasion I was delivering to a Haunted Castle in Bracknell. It was pouring with rain, and I happened to walk past an amusement arcade booth on the fairground. The ground underfoot was muddy, and the torrential downpour caused me to take shelter inside the booth for a few minutes. Naturally, the showman-proprietor came over to see what I was carrying and engaged me in conversation. He bemoaned the fact that business was bad (it always is for travelers, or so they claim!), even though his little amusement arcade seemed packed to the rafters with damp punters eager to shove their pennies into the greedy slots.

I noticed that quite of a few of his slot machines were still taking the old pennies, and had not been converted to the new decimal 1p coins. (This was just a couple of years after Britain converted to decimal currency). The punters had to change their money at the change desk into the old currency to use these machines. I asked him why this was the case, and he said the machines were so old and obsolete that parts to convert them were not made. As it turned out, the row of six "one armed bandits" (or "fruit-machines") had been made in America in the 1940's. But the punters were avidly playing them, and inserting their coins and pulling down the handles with hopeful fervour. He asked me if I knew of anyone who could convert them for him.

My mind flashed back to the little workshop in the Casino in Great Yarmouth where I had watched the mechanic repairing the slot machines there several years earlier. Although complicated devices, they were completely mechanical, so I thought that it should be possible to examine their workings and unravel their mysteries. So I said to the showman "I can do it for you!" even though I didn't have a clue how.

At the time I was living with my parents in their rather genteel middle-class bungalow just outside nearby Wokingham. The showman said he'd deliver the slot machines to me when the fair pulled-down and moved on from Bracknell to Uxbridge the following Sunday. Little did the people of Pine Drive know what was about to arrive in their very quiet and conservative neighbourhood. Travelling fairs move around the country in convoys so that if there are any breakdowns or incidents en-route they can all help one-another. Consequently, although only one vehicle from the showman in question needed to arrive outside my parents bungalow to deliver the six slot machines, the entire fair turned up in the street – "Dodgems on Tour" proclaimed two of the enormous lorries – "Sedgefield's Gigantic Waltzer" was emblazoned on another – "All for your Delight, Perkins Octopus" on another. More and more vehicles entered the street. Net curtains behind the windows of the little bungalows started to twitch. What was arriving in their decent, quiet, law-abiding community?

The machines were duly off-loaded, and the fair departed in a roar of engines and clouds of thick black diesel exhaust. What on earth was happening at the Wardleys' bungalow, people must have thought?

I got the six heavy "one-armed bandits" into the garage, and opened up the backs. The machines were indeed very ancient, and the mechanisms were covered in a thick layer of black dust and grease. To give you a quick insight into the working of slot machines, the coin-handling is divided into two completely separate parts – (1) the coin acceptor/rejector and (2) the payout mechanism. The coin acceptor/rejector is the part immediately inside the slot, and decides if the coin you've inserted is valid, and if so allows the machine to operate. The coin then travels into the payout mechanism, which dispenses the coins in an accurate way according to how much you've won. When its reservoir is full of coins, any surplus falls into the cash box as profit.

On examining the first machine, I could clearly see where the acceptor/rejector was located, but could find no sign of a payout mechanism. I looked at the second machine. The same was true. And of the third, fourth, fifth and sixth. I started to dismantle one of the machines. Not only was there no payout mechanism, it was very obvious that there never could have been one, and indeed the slot machine had been designed such that it would have been impossible to fit one in anyway. So what happened if a punter got a winning combination? The three rotating wheels on the machine had 20 symbols on them – the traditional plums, cherries, oranges and bells. But I noticed that the ratchet cogs that caused the wheels to stop, one at a time, only had 10 positions on them. All the winning combinations were where the wheels could not stop. The money from the slots fell directly into the cash box! Nobody had ever won a single penny from any of these machines during their entire 30 year operational lives!

I was horrified. There was no way I was going to be party to this kind of deception. I reassembled all six machines having done nothing to them. The showman was somewhere near Uxbridge with the fair that week, but there was no means of contacting him (mobile phones were 25 years away in the future), so all I could do was wait until he returned the next Sunday.

Sure enough, on the Sunday afternoon the fair returned to Pine Drive in a cloud of diesel fumes and roar of engines. I was expecting trouble when I told the showman I hadn't touched his machines. I explained to him that there were no payout mechanisms in any of them, and that they were a swindle. His reply was this:

"They have only taken a few pennies off each of my punters, which they can well-afford to lose. But in return they have brought much anticipation and fun to people over the years. But you're a lad with much integrity. And I admire that." And with that, we shook hands and he left. I cannot subscribe to his views, but this was all part of the learning process.

Sometimes I would despair at how some of the travelling showmen made a complete mockery of the term "showman". One in particular, whom I will not mention by name as his offspring are still travelling the same attraction, built and toured a large travelling ghost train that had absolutely nothing inside other than a badly-paint fluorescent face on one of the walls. Punters went in with great anticipation at the horrors within, and came out bored, disappointed and swindled. I offered to supply and install some effects at cost, but he just didn't seem to understand the total inadequacies of his "show".

If I had any gaps to fill between working on films I still performed my illusion act from time-to-time. One of the tricks was when I was put in handcuffs, sealed in an airtight plastic bag (don't try this at home, children, as it is very dangerous) which was then locked in a steel box, and I had just 45 seconds to escape before I suffocated to death (or so the audience was told!). This is what the audience saw:

An assistant would put me in handcuffs and help me into the bag. Another assistant would seal the top of the bag and they would then lift this into the steel box. The lid would be put on the box and loads of padlocks and chains would secure the lid on. Then two more assistants would come on stage with a big screen that was put around the box to hide it from the audience. A large "countdown" clock at the side of the stage was started, and the audience would wait with baited breath to see if I would escape (within 45 seconds) or die. The clock ticked away. 30 seconds. 40 seconds. No sign of movement from behind the screen. 45 seconds, 50, one minute.

Something had gone wrong. After one minute 15 seconds an assistant came on stage looking worried. More assistants rushed on and pulled away the screen. They forced off the box lid, and …. the box was empty! "Where is he?" shouted an assistant. On that cue, I would burst through the entrance doors at the back of the audience, waving the handcuffs above my head and shouting "I'm here!" as I ran down through the audience towards the stage.

How was it done? Very simple really.

As soon as I was concealed inside the bag I could release the trick handcuffs. The moment the lid was put on the box I slit open the bag with the hidden Stanley knife in my pocket, and opened a trapdoor in the back of the box. I unzipped the one-piece stage costume I had on, and underneath I was wearing black trousers and black sweater which matched the stage assistants' clothes. As the screens were put around I got out of the box, now hidden by the screens. The audience were far too busy watching the countdown clock being started to realise that although four assistants had walked onstage to help with the trick, five assistants walked offstage into the shadows backstage. All I then had to do was run through the stage door, back to the front of the theatre and await my cue to burst into the auditorium with as much noise as possible.

One day we were performing the show in a large multipurpose civic centre in the West Midlands. The show was going well, but when I started to run through the stage door to get to the back of the auditorium I got lost in a maze of corridors. When I eventually got to the entrance door of the theatre, I knew it had taken me longer than the allotted time and I had missed my cue, so I just burst through the doors waving my handcuffs above my head and shouting "I'm here".

What I didn't realise was that this civic centre had two theatres within it. One contained our show, and the other hosted the annual convention of the National Association of Knitwear Manufacturers. I had mistaken this for our theatre. Imagine the delegates' surprise when a shouting lunatic burst into their conference waving handcuffs whilst they were in the middle of a riveting talk entitled "The Application of Polymer Yarns in Elasticated Sportswear".

That's Showbusiness!

My first experience of the circus
Bertram Mills Circus 1953 with Mum, Dad and a cat

On the beach at Clacton with Mum
(note the pier in the background, with "Steel Stella" rollercoaster)

My Great Yarmouth landlady "Miss Bond" – 1966
(with me dressed for my Bingo duties)

John as "Milly the Filly"
in "Babes in the Wood" Theatre Royal Windsor 1969

The Crazy Car, built for the Theatre Royal Windsor pantomime 1970

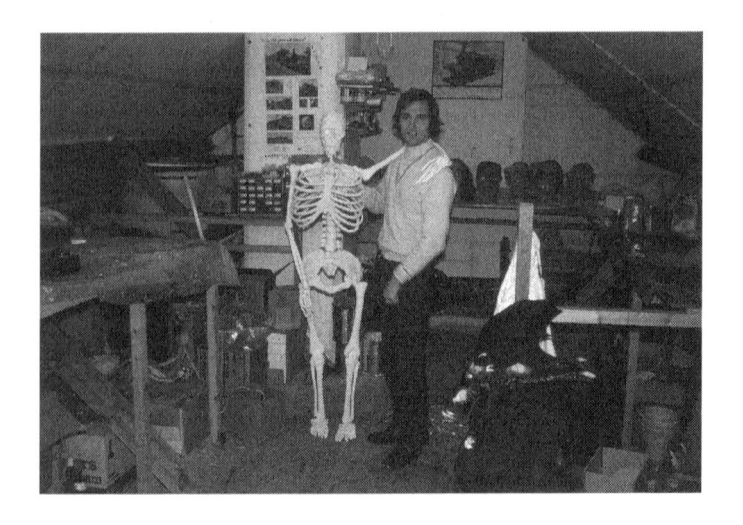

The first dummy skeleton off the production line

In 1974 I received an order from Barry Island Pleasure Park for a gorilla suit (which I had added to my range of standard products) and six skeletons. The previous year, the park's owners, brothers John and Pat Collins, decided that the huge wooden scenic railway at their South Wales amusement park was to be demolished. It had occupied a very large proportion of the total area of the park since its opening in 1940, and as a consequence, after its removal a gigantic hole was left in the park's entertainment offering. The scenic railway was an identical twin brother to the rollercoaster I had ridden as trainee brakeman at Great Yarmouth as a kid, and it had been a big money-earner at Barry Island for many years, but the land it freed-up after its removal could potentially earn far more with other new attractions.

Collins Brothers had turned to an American designer, Alan Hawes, to create a Jungle Boat Ride that was developed at the lower end of the old scenic railway site. The upper end became the site of a small modern rollercoaster, and the middle portion became the location of a large children's dark ride "The Magic Island" with nursery-rhyme scenes created by the park's very talented resident artist, Norman Pratt. That still left space for a number of other attractions including a Haunted Castle, Crazy Cottage, various kiddy rides and side stalls.

The South Wales climate didn't lend itself to the growth of lush tropical jungle foliage, and the animation mechanisms of the fibreglass animals soon rusted-up and became moribund. John and Pat needed to inject some instant life and atmosphere into this expensive new investment, and this is where I came in.

I was still working on the filming of the last few special effects shots of 'The Man with the Golden Gun' at Pinewood Studios when the order arrived from Barry Island. John Collins had the idea of dressing someone up in a gorilla suit and they would leap out at the passing boats near the end of the ride and give the passengers a scare. This animation method required nothing more than large quantities of beer and hotdogs to keep it running. In addition, a few skeletons draped around the rather sparse foliage might add to the exotic atmosphere. So he ordered the gorilla suit and six skeletons which he would collect from me (according to my diary) on the 17th. August.

It turned out that on that particular day I was due to work on the Funhouse set at Pinewood in the afternoon. John Collins arrived to collect his skeletons in the morning and asked what I did (apart from making skeletons and gorilla costumes). I explained that I worked in film special effects and was due to be at Pinewood later that day to work on, of all things, a fairground funhouse scene. He expressed considerable interest (he had his own Funhouse at Barry Island), so I said he could come with me and watch the action. I smuggled him onto the set and he witnessed some Bond filming taking place. From then on we became the best of friends (and he was the best man at my wedding many years later).

A few days after his Bond experience he phoned me up and asked if I would be interested in completely refurbishing an old double-decker ghost train at Barry Island Pleasure Park. Having seen the rather sad and unimaginative ghost trains that travelling showmen toured around the country, I had always wanted to create a fast and furious 'Larf in the Dark' ghost train. As the years had gone by, many operators had removed the effects from their dark rides because of vandalism. Riders tended to vandalise ghost train effects because the cars were slow (hence the riders could easily jump out, or lean out, and smash up the effects), and the rides were boring and amateurish, which left the riders in a frame of mind to abuse them all the more. I was convinced that if the ride was fast, disorientating, and packed full of well-made robust and entertaining effects, it would not get vandalised. But I needed someone with the vision to help me see this through, and John Collins seemed the ideal person..

But although this was something that really appealed to me, I had been approached to work on the special effects of another film at Shepperton Studios immediately after the filming of 'The Man with the Golden Gun' had ended at Pinewood. This film had the working title of "Star Beast" (which, during filming, was subsequently changed to "Alien", and the rest is history!). After much thought I took the bold step of declining this film and arranged to go down to Barry Island to meet up with John and Pat Collins to discuss their project instead. It was a miserable wet Monday morning when I drove along the M4 towards South Wales. At Bristol I put a random tape into the cassette player. It was the Carpenter's Greatest Hits, and Karen Carpenter very appropriately started to sing "Rainy Days and Mondays always get me down". I was beginning to think I had made a big mistake. I was giving up a very well-paid and lucrative career in the film industry to move into a declining branch of the entertainment business, that of the seaside amusement park, in the hope that I could in some small way help to turn around its fortunes.

But as I paid my toll and crossed over the Severn Bridge into Wales the sun came out. Karen was singing "Top of the World", and my spirits lifted. As my car emerged from the Newport tunnels, she sang

"We've Only Just Begun" and something told me that I was about to embark on something very special indeed.

As I descended the hill in Barry towards the sea I caught my first glimpse of Barry Island, with its enormous Butlin's holiday camp as a backdrop to the Pleasure Park. I found the office and was greeted by a jovial John Collins who introduced me to his brother Pat. We looked at the old ghost train, and I outlined my conviction that a big, fast ride full of well-designed effects would disgorge the exiting riders in an animated state which would in turn attract more punters to follow them. John and I discussed this, and he said it was worth a try. John was a very forward-thinking man, who, although brought up within a traditional showman's family, was prepared to move with the times. He also had tremendous generosity of spirit, a kind nature, and a great sense of fun.

The first thing I felt we had to do was to make the ride flat on one level. The slow grind of the cars up the ramps took all the pace and disorientation out of the old two-storey ride, the dip in the middle was rather tame compared to the rollercoaster across the park, and the descents back to ground level were a safety nightmare. The existing building was big enough to pack a huge amount of track into it on one level, and the cars could be speeded up to belt around the circuit at high speed.

One feature I also felt should be built into the ride was that it should emerge back out into the open at least once (and preferably twice) during the course of the ride. This was to provide a spectacle for the riders waiting to board (and arouse the curiosity of spectators undecided as to whether or not to ride). This had been done on ghost trains before, but I felt it important to precede each emergence with a shock effect just before the riders came into view, so that they would be reacting in a dynamic way when they were seen by the spectators.

I measured the building, noted the track geometry of the old ride (in particular the radius of the bends the cars could negotiate) and set-to at the drawing board to create a track layout plan.

I made sure I allowed sufficient room for effects, and where these were within reach of the riders I determined that they should be built in such a robust way that they would be impervious to assault from those with mischievous intent (and some were designed in such a way that if malicious riders did try to vandalise them, it was the riders who came off worst!).

The old ride building was gutted, the floor made level, and the Pleasure Park team (led by Len Smith, Len Marsh, and brothers Jack and Albert Holland) laid the new track. We tested the cars, and they went round the circuit a treat. Even when we speeded them up (and the rear wheels skidded round the bends!) it was obvious we still had a good long ride.

Before the labyrinth of partitions were put in I designed the effects, but I'll talk about these in more detail later.

John Collins and I were convinced we should not call the ride a Ghost Train, and we needed a different image altogether. John's brother Pat was not so sure. To him a Ghost Train was a Ghost Train, and that's what it should be called, but he agreed that if we could come up with something better he'd go along with it. I have always tried to design my rides to have the widest appeal, and believe that although mystery, surprise and the occasional fright are perfectly acceptable, I am dead against sheer horror and depravity. For this reason we wanted to come up with an unusual name that would arouse curiosity in the visitors to the park, and then give the outside of the ride an appropriate façade. The name "Scream Machine" seemed to fit the bill, and a design that gave the appearance of a gigantic mechanism with revolving cogs, reciprocating levers, and smoking chimneys seemed to appeal.

But the concept was still missing something. We needed to take the aggressive edge off the ride and make it family-friendly without losing the teenage appeal and the spooky theme. So this is where I came up with the idea of Uncle Frankenstein. We would create a large animated friendly-looking monster with a smiling face and welcoming demeanor who would stand high up on the façade to draw the crowds. I commissioned Mike and Janet Blackman from Chichester to sculpt and mould the character, and a local engineering company to produce its animation mechanism.

The British public were wary of traditional dark rides that had spectacular facades promising all sorts of thrills within, only to find a dark empty booth that the trains trundled round, ejecting rather bored and dissatisfied riders at the exit. In fact the German 'Geisterbahns' are mainly still like this, with incredibly elaborate and ornate facades, and virtually nothing inside. Instead, we would use the façade to draw the crowds to the ride, but let the riders themselves be the show on the front. We would ensure that everyone who got off the ride was the greatest advocate in persuading others to go on. To this end, considerable effort was put into conceiving the effects that assaulted you just a few seconds before you emerged from the two sets of mid-course doors and the final exit doors. Hence, the interior effects would have the lion's share of the budget, and the façade the bare minimum. It was a risky tactic, but John and Pat had the confidence in me that I could make it work.

So the façade was quite minimal, with a plain black background, huge white letters bearing the words "Scream Machine", revolving silver cogs, metal chimneys, and, of course, the large Uncle Frankenstein figure. I composed the lyrics of a song (inspired to a large degree by the song "Monster Mash"), edited some music as a backing track and found a penniless actor at the Redgrave Theatre in Farnham to record it, and this accompanied Uncle Frankenstein's gyrations on the front of the attraction. And at the same time, a motley team of people all over the country were creating the interior effects for us.

And now I'll let you into the secret of just what the riders of Uncle Frankenstein's Scream Machine experienced…

The cars went through a pair of double doors that formed a light lock, and took a sharp right-hand bend. Sinister laughter could be heard in the pitch darkness. A glowing skull appeared ahead and rapidly moved towards the car whizzing close over the heads of the riders, and screaming as it went. This effect (which can also still be seen in Blackpool Pleasure Beach's fabulous Ghost Train) was achieved by suspending a long run of heavy-duty overhead sliding door track from the ceiling, pivoted about a centre point, and tipped first in one direction then the other by a pneumatic cylinder. The UV painted skull was attached to a runner in the track, and, as the car approached, the track tipped slightly downwards towards the approaching car, and after the skull had passed over the heads of the riders the track would tip in the other direction and return it back to its starting point. The skull was within reach of the riders, but anyone with malicious intent would discover the whole thing was built like a chieftain tank and if they tried to grab it or punch it, their knuckles would be grazed or their shoulders ripped out of their sockets. The local yobs soon began to realise that you don't mess with the Scream Machine!

The next effect was a skeleton prisoner chained to a brick wall, who writhed and yelled as you passed. This had to be protected by a unbreakable polycarbonate sheet, which was always kept polished and the effect was lit in such a way that the protective glazing was not visible.

Again, if you leaned out of the car to grab it, you got a very nasty shock (and a bruised forehead!).

After this there were a series of dark bends where you then encountered a giant (4m tall) monster brandishing a massive club. He brought this club violently down supposedly on your head as you passed. This figure used the same fibreglass body moulds as Uncle Frankenstein, but with a different head.

The next effect was to my mind the best of the whole ride, and something that was completely baffling and disorientating. Many other park operators who rode the Scream Machine would ask us how we did it, but (with one exception) we never revealed the secret. (That one exception was my dear friend, the late Geoffrey Thompson, owner of Blackpool Pleasure Beach, whose kindness and generosity to me meant I couldn't deny him the secret). This is what seemed to happen: a skeleton appeared to leap out in front of the car and jump up and down. You swerved to narrowly miss it and were confronted by a second skeleton. You swerved to miss this and there was a third! But this time you didn't swerve out of the way: you hit it, and it blasted apart, with its arms and legs flying in all directions. The effect was amazing and something that people still talk to me about. How was it done? Simple...

You have probably seen that when things are illuminated by strobe lights, they appear to move even if they are static. As long as you (the observer) are moving, the object being lit by the strobe takes on a life of its own. I discovered that if you put a piece of special black glass (known in the trade as "Wood's glass") in front of a strobe light, it removes all the visible light and turns it into a UV black light strobe. The skeletons were low-relief fibreglass panels fixed to the wall. The mould that produced the three sets of panels had three sets of arms and legs, so that different poses could be produced by painting different limbs in fluorescent paint and leaving others painted black. Two of the panels were fixed to the walls that the cars narrowly dodged, but the third was irregularly cut along a zigzag line down the middle and fixed to a pair of doors that the cars hit and burst through. But the real secret of the apparent animation was the use of the black light strobes, which gave about three or four flashes of intense UV light to each skeleton as you approached it. The effect was simple, vandal-proof, but very effective. And people were convinced the skeletons actually moved!

The doors on which the last skeleton was located were the first pair of the light lock leading out into the first exterior loop of track, so it was necessary to do something fairly diabolical to the riders to make them react as they emerged into view of the spectators. Nothing sophisticated here, just a blast of water spray and compressed air from a spray nozzle at the side of the track at face height. It was guaranteed to make even the toughest visitor react in just the way we wanted. Everyone emerged with their hands in front of their faces looking very surprised or laughing helplessly. And then as soon as they had come out they were spun straight back in again for the second section of the ride.

The effect they then encountered was none other than Uncle Frankenstein who popped his head up from behind a low wall in front of the track. Then round a couple more bends a massive hairy caveman tried to roll a large rock over onto the track ahead from an elevated ledge. Just before the second exterior loop, the reaction we needed this time was caused by a stack of four wooden crates, piled precariously on top of each other, which wobbled and toppled over in front of the car. This was obviously going to be a potential safety hazard, and the park's resident engineer, Len Marsh, built a very solid steel articulated framework within, and heavy safety chains to restrain the boxes should they really fall in the event of the mechanism failing. During the ride's life, this (and the other effects) operated over one million cycles, with never a problem.

And then it was back out into the daylight, and straight back in again for the final section of the ride.

The riders were assaulted by some loud noises, and then a hanging man dropped down from above in front of the car. Then the final effect. Again, we needed something that was guaranteed to produce an emotive reaction on the emerging riders. The car appeared to pass along a corridor through a series of archways supported by pillars continuing on into the distance. Halfway along this colonnade the car seemed to derail, swerve first slightly to the left, then to the right, and crash into one of the columns and then through the brick wall behind. This was accompanied by strobe flashes and suitably very loud sound effects. In the ensuing apparent chaos a second brick wall was hit, and the car immediately burst into the daylight and the safety of the exit.

Uncle Frankenstein's Scream Machine was a huge hit. It operated at full capacity from 10 in the morning till 10 at night all over the Easter holiday period, with long queues forming outside, and it continued to thrill visitors to Barry Island Pleasure Park for many years to come. I had intended to stay down in Barry to keep an eye on the ride for just one more week after Easter, but much more was to follow.

Chapter 9

PROFESSIONAL SUICIDE?

"You've got to be joking!" my special effects colleagues in the film studios told me. "You're turning down valuable work at the studios to build tacky ghost trains in funfairs in South Wales. Have you gone mad?"

Perhaps I had, but I was loving the immediacy of the work I was doing. The punters paid their money, you gave them a thrill. If you succeeded they went straight to the back of the queue, and rode again. If you didn't, you got a punch in the face. What could be more down to earth than that!

And I had a vision ... Sometime in the future I would develop the theme park concept in Britain, and I would use Barry Island to learn my craft and prepare the way.

After the Scream Machine opened, John Collins asked me if I might be able to help redesign the animated animals in the Jungle Boat ride, particularly the underwater crocodiles which were supposed to lunge at the boats as they passed, and the basking hippos that loomed up out of the water. I had done some underwater pneumatics for a rather low-budget horror film at Bray Studios a few years previously, and knew the techniques and pitfalls to a reliable mechanism. So I got the creatures back to my workshops and rebuilt them. They were re-installed, and worked fine. By this time, the poor lad in the gorilla suit had had enough and I was asked if I could make it a totally mechanical animated effect, needing neither beers nor hotdogs to keep it working.

But we were concerned that this effect of the gorilla jumping out of the box at the end of the ride left a lot of little children crying and screaming as they emerged from the exit. This in turn put off young families from going on. So I suggested a rather surreal twist. The wooden crate, with the words "Dangerous Wild Animal Inside" stencilled on the side, would be mounted on a little jetty that the boats would pass immediately next to. The crate would be violently shaking, and loud growling noises would come from within. Just as the boat passed in front of it, the front would burst open, and there was a cute little teddy bear sat inside.

Now, this sounds a pretty stupid idea. But we built it exactly like that, and it worked a treat. Everyone was prepared for something very horrific and nasty to happen when they passed the box, and they were forced to laugh at themselves when their fears proved unjustified.

One day John Collins came up to me. "Do you know anything about turns?" he said. "Turns? What sort of turns?" I asked. "You know, like fire-eaters and knife-throwers and other kinds of , well , turns."

He explained that getting people into the park in the middle of the summer season on Friday evenings was proving a real problem. The nearby holiday camp did everything they could to extract the last penny out of the holidaymakers' pockets on their final evening before they returned home on the Saturday. They ran free bingo, cheap booze, competitions with cash prizes. You name it, and they did it to stop the campers leaving on Friday evening and spending their money elsewhere. Barry Island Pleasure Park suffered as a consequence. John wanted to fight fire with fire (or, rather, fire-eaters). So we decided that Friday nights would be Carnival Night, with a disco, cheap prices on the rides, and ..... TURNS!

There was no stage on the Pleasure Park, so a trailer from an old artic truck was found somewhere on Barry docks, towed to the park, and set up next to the Funhouse. It was just the right size and height for a stage. Norman Pratt made some lovely scenery as a backdrop, painted like a magic fairytale castle, and Len Marsh rigged up some lights. A local disco was hired for the season to provide the sound and music. The only task left was booking the turns. We approached an agent in Bristol who assured us he could supply a different novelty act every week for the next ten weeks. The first week, an excellent comedy trampoline act called the Tumblairs arrived, who went down really well. The following week, a strongman who called himself "The Mighty Strang" did amazing things with a length of steel pipe and two cannon balls.

The third week we were promised "Kady and Partner" Britain's only female knife-thrower and sharp-shooter. The publicity leaflet the agent sent in advance had a photo of a very glamorous young lady in cow-girl costume, throwing knives and aiming a rifle at her young male assistant. The Friday evening crowds were going to love this. We reproduced their photo on posters around the park.

At about 6 o'clock in the evening of that particular Friday, I was in the pleasure park office and I heard a loud bang come from the staff car park outside, and a cloud of black smoke drifted past the window. I looked out, and saw that an extraordinary-looking vehicle (which had the appearance of a converted Mr. Whippy icecream-van-turned-into-a-mobile-home) had pulled up in the car park, and had violently backfired. Out stepped a rather stooped elderly lady from the passenger seat, and an equally mature gentleman with a pronounced limp from the driver's side. Terrible thoughts started going through my mind. I glanced at Kady and Partner's publicity photo. Could this be ...? Oh no, please God, don't let it be.

But it was.

The publicity photo had obviously been taken of them about 100 years earlier. And we were about to see this geriatric couple throwing knives and firing rifles around a crowded amusement park. A mass-execution could be about to take place. I was tempted to phone for an ambulance there and then.

They came to the office window, and Mr. Webber, the quiet and gentle office manager, announced to us "The turn's arrived". I showed them into the dressing room (well, a store room for the bingo "swag" actually) and they then proceeded to unload from their Mr. Whippy conversion an alarming assortment of weapons that, if got into the wrong hands, could arm a revolution. The couple were the sweetest people, and I tried to receive them in a welcoming and warm manner, hoping my concern and disappointment was not showing through.

Mr. Webber reappeared. "Mr. Wardley," (he always addressed me as Mr. Wardley, since Christian names didn't exist in his respectful world) "Can you go over to the Scream Machine quickly. Uncle Frankenstein's developed an alarming squeak, and old Tom is worried its about to seize up."

There was nothing for it, but to let fate take its course. I left Kady and Partner to prepare for their performance and headed for the Scream Machine to attend to the huge animated Frankenstein figure that decorated its facade. There was nothing seriously wrong that a quick squirt of oil couldn't sort out. I unzipped its flies, inserted the nozzle of the oilcan, and gave it a good dose of lubricant, much to the amazement of the people queueing for the ride.

An hour later, it was SHOW-TIME!

An enormous crowd had gathered in front of the stage, as Disco Dick did his warm-up act. "And now ladies and gentlemen, boys and girls, Barry Island Pleasure Park proudly presents, direct from the Wild West ..." (*Oh, for goodness sake Dick, get on with it*) ... "Kady and Partner".

I braced myself for the worst. There was a pause as their recorded music (Doris Day's "Whip Crack Away") blasted out:

> *Oh the Deadwood Stage is a-rollin' on over the plains*
> *With the curtains flappin' and the driver slappin' the reins*
> *A beautiful sky, a wonderful day*
> *Whip crack-away, whip crack-away, whip crack-away*

And then an incredible apparition appeared on stage. An attractive lady accompanied by a very smart guy, both dressed in Western costume, bounded on. She was cracking a whip with deafening effect, as he leaped onto a small dais and stood next to a board with his outline painted on it.

I couldn't believe my eyes. Surely the illusion wasn't achieved just through make-up and costumes? Yes, it was! And sheer charismatic stage professionalism. They looked fantastic! Knives flew through the air and impaled themselves into the board a hair's breadth away from "Partner"'s body (his name turned out to be Ernie). Rifle bullets shot through targets balanced on his head, and cigarettes held in his mouth were whipped in half with a resounding crack. Perhaps my nickname for their mode of transport was not inappropriate after all.

The act was a resounding success, and the crowds applauded and applauded.

After the show, John, Pat and I thanked them profusely. It proved to me that you can never go by backstage appearances in the magical world of showbusiness. That was yet another lesson I learnt which proved invaluable.

The next week an illusionist was booked, and his first trick was to show a box empty, and then out would pop his young lady assistant. Obviously, she was put in the box backstage, and Disco Dick and I had to wheel the box onto the stage (with the girl inside) and then the magician was to be announced and would come on stage. Unfortunately, nobody had realised that two of the tyres on our artic-lorry trailer stage had gone flat, and the stage had developed a very slight slope from back to front. No sooner had we put the box in position and turned our back on it, than the thing started to slowly roll downstage towards the audience. It picked up speed, and before we could grab it, it slide off the front of the stage into the crowd, smashed open on the tarmac ground, out shot the poor girl in floods of tears, and ran off (never to be seen again). The helpless illusionist had to terminate his performance. But the crowd seemed to enjoy it, and thought that was the act!

But the calibre of the acts really started to diminish week by week from here on in, as the agent was running out of novelty turns to provide. The escapologist one week was so bad (and I think 30 years later they are still trying to get him out of that padlocked milkchurn) that I phoned up the agent and said we weren't happy paying for such rubbish. He got quite aggressive on the phone, and said we'd signed a contract with him. So I told him exactly which of his bodily orifices he could stick his contract up, and hung up the phone. (I saw the agent the following year at a convention, and judging by the way he was walking, it looked as if he'd taken my advice very literally.)

Then John Collins uttered the fateful words "You used to do a turn, didn't you, John?"

There was nothing for it. We were in a right pickle, and I knew that my act was far better than the appalling turns that the agent had been recently giving us, and charging us a fortune for. So I got all my illusion props out of store, rehearsed Debbie from the Dodgems to be my lovely assistant, and for the rest of that summer season we became the Friday Carnival Night turn. And, secretly, I have to admit that I rather enjoyed it.

The money we were saving in not paying for speciality acts allowed us to buy from America a fabulous levitation illusion to add to our act. This was air-freighted in, and was a brilliant piece of engineering. Unlike most conventional levitation illusions, this could be performed in the open air, away from a backcloth, in broad daylight. Debbie would be placed on a board between two trestles, the trestles would be removed, and up she'd float. A hoop would be passed all around her to prove there were no wires or other means of support, then she'd continue her upward journey. As I've previously mentioned, the stage was located next to the large two-storey Funhouse on the park, which had windows on the upper floor through which the occupants could look out as they negotiated the labyrinth within.

I noticed some of the local lads would go into the Funhouse when we were about to do the trick, and hang around at this window, looking down on the stage from this elevated viewpoint in the hope that they could see how the levitation worked. The device was so clever that this was futile. But it occurred to me that if we made a big thing about trying to clear the spectators from this viewpoint before we did the illusion, it might actually encourage more punters to pay to go in. So Disco Dick would announce "For the next amazing illusion, we would like to ask all of you up at the Funhouse window to please come down to watch the show". This had the desired effect, as dozens of people flocked to the Funhouse turnstile proffering their 75p's, in the hope that they could find out the secret of Debbie's flight.

Whilst working on projects at Barry Island I was involved in various advisory committees for the Wales Tourist Board, assessing the viability of applications for grant aid for developing tourist attractions. One of these was Llechwedd Slate Caverns at Blaenau Ffestiniog in North Wales. This underground attraction took visitors on a small narrow-gauge mine train deep into the heart of the mountain where they could view the slate mine workings. But it had a problem brought about by its success. The single track train had very limited capacity, and queues on busy days during the peak summer months were sometimes three hours long. Something needed to be done, and I was asked to help.

The mine workings at Llechwedd were enormous, and extended to sixteen different levels in the mountain which, from top to bottom, were taller than the Eiffel Tower. They had been disused and abandoned for over seventy years. The current tour went horizontally from the valley bottom at Level 8. There were eight more levels going into the mountainside above, and another seven levels deep below the valley floor, accessed by an inclined shaft. These lower levels had been allowed to flood and were totally underwater. Ian Rutherford was the managing director of the tour company, and I arranged to go up to North Wales to the site to meet him. It was immediately apparent that the existing tour could not be expanded in capacity, so we needed to find a way to create a new tour through one of the other levels.

He reasoned that if we could build a funicular railway down the incline from the valley floor, we could create a circular walking route through the caverns so that several groups could be on the tour at any one time, and the funicular would shuttle the visitors up and down to the surface. However, as these levels were completely flooded, we had to rely on very ancient plans of the underground passages and tunnels, and the memories of some of the (also very ancient!) retired miners who had worked down there as boys and still lived in the local town. These memories were extracted from the old miners by plying them with vast quantities of beer in the local pubs, and hoping that the alcohol would not distort the accuracy of their recollections, or render their thick Welsh accents even more unintelligible than they were when sober.

But the only way we could accurately assess whether a circular underground pedestrian route could be achieved was to pump out the millions of gallons of water that flooded the mine, and go down and explore. Since the old pumps were completely useless, there was nothing for it but to bring in some massive new pumps at enormous expense. After much deliberation by the company owners, this was agreed, and pumping started.

Day by day, inch by inch, the water level dropped. After about three weeks of continuous pumping, Ian phoned me to say that the water should be down to the floor of Level 7 (the first level down from the surface) by the following day. I jumped in my car and drove the four hour drive up to Llechwedd.

The next morning, Ian and I donned mining overalls and helmets, and descended the steep incline into the abandoned mine. Within a few feet of the surface we were entering a world that no-one had been able to go into for over seventy years. After a couple of hundred feet, passageways led off the incline to the left and right, whilst ahead was the inky black surface of the remaining water. The pumps had done their job, and the mine was now accessible throughout Level 7. With considerable trepidation we started to explore. If the plans were right, we should be able to find our way around the level via the passage to the right, and emerge around the 900-yard circular route back out from the passage to the left.

Submerged for seventy years, this underground world was very eerie. Rotting remnants of old ladders, rusting tools, mine trucks and other abandoned artifacts littered the passageways. Just as the plan had predicted, at times the small passage opened out into vast cathedral-like caverns where the bulk of the slate had been excavated. All seemed to be going according to plan. But then, without warning, ahead of us we found our way was blocked by what looked like a large puddle. Further investigation with our low-powered helmet-mounted mining lamps showed that we were standing on the bank of an enormous underground lake that stretched off into the distance as far as we could see. This was not what we had predicted.

After a few moments thought, Ian worked out what had happened. Over the years, the ceiling of the cavern in the level below had collapsed, and as we had only pumped down to the level we were standing on, the lake we were seeing was the water flooding the mine below us. In theory, if we re-traced our steps back to the incline, and then went through the other passage to trace the route backwards, we should come out on the other side of this lake. But how would we know it was the same lake? We decided that I should stay put where I was, and Ian would go back around the route. I sat alone in the darkness for what seemed like an eternity, surrounded by the ghosts of the old miners. It was a most un-nerving experience. But then, way across the lake, I saw a light flickering in the darkness, and a voice called out. It was Ian, and his theory had worked. We estimated that the lake was over 150 feet across; far too much to bridge. What could be done?

We returned to the surface somewhat dejected. The only thing to do was to carry on pumping. If we could pump down to Level 6, perhaps we could find a circular route down through that level. So the pumps were started up again.

Another three weeks, and another phone call. The water was down now to Level 6 and we could carry out further exploration. We re-traced our route along Level 7 up as far as where the lake had been, but now we were confronted by a sheer drop of around 60 feet where the floor had given way. Using ropes and ladders we clambered down the cliff and found ourselves standing on the floor of Level 6. Using the sketchy plans, we explored the passageways of this level which led back to the same incline, but further down.

Success! We had discovered a circular route for the new tour. Steps could be easily built to get the visitors down the cliff face, and the funicular railway (which was subsequently installed) would drop the visitors off at the upper level, and pick them back up at the lower level. A sophisticated audio-visual presentation was created that led the visitors through the tunnels, using sound and light to draw the groups from one cavern to another, as the story of the old mine was dramatically told. Princess Margaret came to do the official opening, and now, over thirty years later, that is what millions of visitors to Llechwedd Slate Caverns have subsequently done (and still do!).

Back at Barry Island, the summer wore on, and towards the end of the season John and Pat Collins asked if I could give some thought to the Magic Island family dark ride, which was proving to be something of a white elephant.

This was housed in a large building halfway down the park. The visitors rode in little bunny-rabbit-shaped cars around the interior of the building through grottos containing animated tableaux of nursery rhyme stories. But it suffered from "World Cruise Syndrome" (remember that, at Battersea Funfair?) where the more adventurous riders took it upon themselves to alight from the moving vehicles, and imaginatively rearrange the tableaux. Never before had Snow White had such a good time with the Seven Dwarfs.

Could I think of any way we could re-use both the building, and the track and cars within, and create a brand new ride?

I had always admired Blackpool Pleasure Beach's Goldmine Ride. Having given Geoffrey Thompson free range to explore the secrets of my Scream Machine dark ride, he agreed to return the compliment and I spent a couple of days crawling around his Goldmine attraction in Blackpool. The theme provided a good reason for an enclosed pseudo-underground environment, the mining aspect gave added appeal, and the gold made it slightly exotic. I vowed we should add yet another layer to this theme – Hillbilly chaos – and the Whacky Goldmine was born!

We took one of the bunny-rabbit cars and built an inclined test track to see if they could climb hills and descend slopes. It turned out that they could. Then we experimented to see if they could climb hills and turn bends at the same time. Not quite so satisfactory, but probably do-able. Using this information I started to design a completely new track layout for the building, and new bodies for the cars were built by a local carpentry firm to give the appearance of wooden mine trucks.

Now, when you go into a mine, you go *down*, normally. Blackpool's ride had the advantage of the station being on an elevated plaza, with the ride descending down several storeys to ground level, giving a splendid illusion of going down a mine. But at Barry Island we didn't have this luxury, so I designed the loading station platform about two metres above ground. The track would enter the building, and descend rapidly while turning a sharp bend. But within about ten meters, the track had reached ground level. How could we keep up the appearance that the track carried on descending into the bowels of the earth for the rest of the ride?

In Scotland there is a place called the Electric Brae. It is on the A719 south of Dunure, not far from Ayr. The road appears to be running uphill, but if a driver stops, goes into neutral, and then takes his foot off the brake, he will coast *uphill*! Obviously, it's an illusion. The road actually slopes downhill, but because of the surrounding features of the landscape, particularly the windblown trees that slope at an angle to the vertical, the driver's sense of horizontality is completely disorientated. The road really does look as if it is going up. Could we do the same in the Whacky Goldmine, but in reverse?

Yes, we could.

Consequently, all the internal scenery, effects and animations in the ride were designed on the tilt, to completely throw the riders off balance. What they assumed was vertical was not vertical. The result was that you really did feel as if you were travelling down and down into the depths of the mine. One effect did give us a problem with this theory, and that was the flood effect where water had to cascade all around. How could we make water slope? The answer was the use of jets that squirted the water at an angle, so that what looked like vertically-falling water was actually angled-squirted water.

Further on in the tour of the mine, I proposed an animated figure of a miner, dangling by one hand from a broken ladder high up in the roof of the mine. He was to shout and scream for help.

I started to construct the figure myself, and got a bit carried away. I purchased a very realistic wax head from Gems Wax Models in London, made a plaster mold from this, and cast a new head in flexible rubber latex. When I put my hand inside, I found that by manipulating the mouth I could produce a very convincing articulation of speech. Vowels and consonants could all be reproduced. My experience in film special effects using miniature pneumatic cylinders to operate small mechanical devices came in handy, and within a few weeks I had produced a very realistic animatronic head that could move its eyes, blink, and articulate speech. Since I had no decent engineering equipment available to me, I had made the mechanism out of bits of door hinges, old springs, bent pieces of tin and wire … in fact it was a real Heath Robinson botch-up, but it worked!

But in the Whacky Goldmine the riders would whizz past my miner in the semi-darkness, and it was obvious that something of this realism and complexity would be completely lost on the audience. So the figure was built with a new head, and animated mouth that opened and closed like a ventriloquist's dummy. And it was perfectly adequate.

We finished building the Whacky Goldmine during the following closed winter season, and at Easter it opened. It was both popular, successful, and profitable. Mission accomplished! Then I went on to design a logflume ride on an impossibly small site, which taught me much about how to coax large volumes of water to swill along winding troughs, propelling boats at high speed up lifts and down chutes.

I'm now going to give you a little lecture on the theory of fluid dynamics when applied to logflumes. If you think this is going to be unbelievably boring, do feel free to skip forward a page. But you never know, you might actually find this interesting.

You would assume that if you built a completely level trough and poured water in one end, it would flow happily along the trough and pour out the other. Well, that might work for a trickle of water, but as you start to pump more and more water into the trough, the friction of the bottom and sides causes the water to build up at the entry end and flood over the sides of the trough. To overcome this, you need to give the trough a gentle downward slope, and the gradient of this slope depends on the volume of water you pump in, the speed you want the water to flow at, the depth of water you want to achieve, and the roughness of the surface of the trough. Concrete trough has a rougher surface than fibreglass trough, so the slope needs to be greater. By altering the roughness of the surface of the trough you can create waves, and by changing the gradient of the trough you can speed the water up and make it more shallow, or slow it down and make it deeper.

Right, that's the boring bit out of the way. So with the Barry Island Logflume we were learning from first principles. The French firm who were going to construct it had only built one logflume ride before, and that was a very slow dreary ride. I wanted the logs to whizz around the trough as fast as possible, so that meant a huge volume of water ...... nearly 1¼ million gallons an hour, to be precise! This is how it's calculated:

(Sorry, here comes another boring bit .... Assume the depth of water is 35 cm., and the width of the trough is 160 cm., that gives a cross sectional area of water of 0.56 sq.m. If the water is to flow at 2.5 m/second, this gives a volume of 1.4 cu.m/second or 1,103,760 gallons per hour).

To be certain we had enough water we purchased pumps of extra capacity, as it's far better to have too much water than too little (and the boats will bottom on the trough, and possibly even stop if they're heavily loaded). So we built the ride, and the day came when we were to test it. The lake which formed the reservoir from which the water was pumped was duly filled (with over half a million gallons of water), and, with great trepidation, the pumps were turned on for the very first time. At first nothing seemed to be happening, other than the sound of a powerful electrical hum coming from the huge electric motors which drove the pumps. Then a great wall of water surged out of the outlets, round the smooth fibreglass elevated trough, and cascaded down the big chute with spectacular force. It hit the bottom of the concrete trough beneath, which started to flood. The water overflowed the trough, and a massive wave surged across the viewing pathway in front of the ride, down the main midway of the park, out of the main entrance and across the road in front of the amusement park.... heading straight for Forte's IceCream Parlour on Paget Road.

Whoops!

"STOP THE PUMPS!" I shouted.

Fortunately, Len Marsh was standing by the pump controls and hit the emergency stop button in the nick of time just as the water was about to merge with Forte's raspberry ripple icecream. It dispersed down some roadside drains outside Crole's Amusement Arcade, and we all breathed a sigh of relief.

Did we have a problem? No. As I said, too little water is the problem with water rides. Too much can be rectified by re-tuning the pump impellers, and fixing stainless steel plates to the concrete trough to reduce the friction and speed up the water. This we did, and the water flowed perfectly. Then by adding gratings and baffles to the base of the trough in specific places we could create waves just where we wanted them. The ride worked perfectly, and the logs floated around just as I'd hoped.

I learnt much from the old Barry Island Logflume, which operated very happily for over 25 years, before the whole park fell into disrepair and became sadly derelict.

But if I was to move forward and really develop serious theme park rides in the future, there was one piece missing from the jigsaw puzzle. I had at my fingertips most of the tools of the trade. I understood how ride transit systems could move large numbers of people around twisting circuits, both in water and on tracks, and I was familiar with the companies in the trade who supplied these. I knew how to build scenery, sets and props. And I understood how to design and create special effects. But what about the cast of characters ... the "personalities" which brought the scenes in the rides to life? Disney used very sophisticated animated figures to populate their various show rides, and they were very secretive about how they worked. And, in those days, nobody else was making them.

There was only one thing for it. I had to do it myself.

I was living at that time in a very draughty flat at the top of the Esplanade Buildings on Barry Island sea front, right next to the Pleasure Park. One of the bedrooms was converted into a workshop, where I turned my attention to the original head I had built for the Whacky Goldmine and had abandoned. I needed to find some way of programming the features in synchronisation with a recorded soundtrack, and this was long before the days when the average person had ever heard of computers and digital electronics. The mouth articulated using three separate miniature pneumatic cylinders, which in turn moved the jaw, upper lip and lower lip of the face. I therefore required at least three switched electric outputs from a tape recorder to achieve this, together with a soundtrack. Then I had a flash (literally!) of inspiration. I was at a disco, and noticed the D.J.'s lights flashed along with the music. The red lights responded to the base notes, the blue lights to the mid-notes, and the green lights to the top-notes.

I bought one of these "sound-to-light" converters, and instead of the output from the three channels powering lights, I connected them to the three solenoid valves that controlled the mouth movements. By making weird beeping noises at different pitches into a microphone, I could make the mouth move. By recording these on one channel of a stereo tape recorder, and a soundtrack on the other I could make the head talk and sing.

I spent many hours experimenting with different recorded songs, and trying to perfect my strangled beeping technique to move the jaw, upper lip and lower lip to form the corresponding words. The result was encouraging enough to give me confidence to move on to the body. I decided I would start off with a seated figure, as this would be easier to animate than one standing. I conceived a figure who would be sitting on a chair, playing a guitar. So again I set-to with door hinges, springs, copper pipe, knicker elastic, and virtually anything that came to hand to create the animated body. Fortunately, nobody would ever see inside either the head or body to find out just how crude it all was. The figure tapped his foot, fingered the guitar's frets, plucked the strings, moved its torso, turned and nodded its head, looked around, blinked ….. and SANG!

But it was all too much for my crude disco sound-to-light converter to control. I needed something much more sophisticated. And then someone told me about a guy at Manchester University who was apparently a genius. The thought of contacting a genius struck me as rather exciting, so I got in touch with him. It turned out that he was at the cutting edge of digital electronics, and he really was a genius. He lived in a stone cottage just outside the isolated village of Kettleshulme (which the locals pronounce like "kettle zoom" … who wouldn't want to live in a village with the delightful-sounding name of Kettle Zoom?!), high up in the Peak District above Macclesfield.

The extraordinary thing about him was that although by day he was working in Manchester at the forefront of electronic technology, his home had no electricity! Not one single volt! This was by choice. There was mains electricity running right past the house, but he, his wife and four children lived in blissful happiness in a home illuminated by oil lamps, heated by open fires, with no television or even a radio. They entertained themselves in the evening by reading the Bible together and singing songs, to the accompaniment of a treadle-operated harmonium. It was like stepping back into a 17th century Puritan home, and on the two occasions I visited them I found the family atmosphere very peaceful and enlightening. In a way, I really admired them.

I explained to him what I wanted, and without any fuss he just got on and did it. Three months later it was finished. A rack of baffling-looking electronic circuit boards, with a front panel containing various switches, sockets and neon indicator lamps. I bought a rather expensive top-of-the-range Revox tape recorder, and he fitted a special recording head onto it, about 5cm. away from the sound heads, so that the digital signals would be played back in advance of the sound. This compensated for the delay which my pneumatic valves produced when they operated the movements.

The tape recorder was plugged into the rack, and the rack connected to the 15 valves that operated the individual movements of the figure's head and body. I could program the figure, one channel at a time, by playing the soundtrack and pressing a button to make the corresponding movement operate. Then the tape would be re-wound, and the next channel programmed whilst playing back the previously programmed movements. Gradually I could build up, layer by layer, a complete performance. Today, one could achieve a control system of this type using an ordinary laptop computer and a piece of standard software. But back in the late 1970's this was cutting-edge technology!

Up to now, I had considered the figure nothing more than a mechanical machine which just happened to resemble a human being. But everyone who saw it would ask me its name, and regarded it as having a personality. So I had to give it a name. Since it was a country-and-western singer playing the guitar, I called it Charlie Pluckett.

Charlie Pluckett
the animated robotic figure

Chapter 10

TOMORROW'S WORLD

With Charlie Pluckett now able to perform, it was necessary to teach him a repertoire of songs. This was a very laborious process, rather like creating an animated cartoon film, frame by frame. But eventually, Charlie was ready for his public debut.

It was vitally important that the means by which he operated was kept a closely-guarded secret. When compressed air had been used to operate animated figures in the past, they tended to have a rather jerky movement as the cylinders out-stroked and came to a rapid stop, then in-stroked and stopped. I had found a way to produce smooth-flowing "ramped" movement, in a rather novel way. I had contacted a patent agent in London to see if I could legally protect my invention, but he advised me that once people found out my technique when the patent was published, they could easily circumvent this. His advice was that I should not divulge the inner workings to anyone.

So I installed the compressor that supplied the compressed air to the valves, in the projection room of the old disused cinema in the same building as my flat. In this way it would not be heard. A pipe went through an adjoining wall to the valves that were housed in an adjacent room to the figure itself. Only a small loom of thin nylon tubes ran through the heel of one of Charlie's boots, up his trouser leg, and then spread out around his body to the various animation cylinders. When he performed, there was not a sound of any mechanical devices to give away the secret of his workings.

Charlie gave concerts in the flat to a few friends and staff of the Pleasure Park. Then the local paper, the Barry and District News, got to hear of it and ran an article with photos. This was picked up by the South Wales Echo, and eventually the local BBC evening news program "Wales Today" got in touch. They asked if I could bring Charlie Pluckett to the BBC Studios in Cardiff. I explained this was not possible, so they agreed to come to us. They filmed a piece for their show, and it was broadcast.

Then things started to seriously snowball! One of the most popular TV shows of the time was a science and technology programme called "Tomorrow's World". It attracted audiences of over 10 million viewers every week. The director somehow saw the BBC Wales piece, and got in touch. He asked the same question: "Can you bring Charlie Pluckett to the Television Centre in London, to be a guest on the show?" This time I said "Yes". I had no idea of how I was going to do it, but somehow I was going to get Charlie and his associated paraphernalia to London. He was going to be a TV star!

The main presenter of the show at that time was a very charismatic young guy called Michael Rodd. He fancied himself as a bit of a singer-songwriter (quite a good one, too), so he composed a song ("Nobody Loves You When You're a Robot") recorded it, and sent it to me to pre-program Charlie to sing and perform. The idea was that the two of them would sing a duet live on National BBC Television … live! … to 10 million viewers!

No. I couldn't risk it. Charlie was generally well-behaved, but at times he could develop a slight twitch, occasionally an eyelid would get stuck down, and one time his left hand fell off mid-song. If something went wrong during the show, I'd never live it down. So I said that I'd only do it if they recorded it for a future week's show. They reluctantly agreed, and a few weeks later I bundled Charlie into a van with his compressor and control equipment and set off up the M4 for London. All things considered, it all went very smoothly. Michael Rodd turned out to be the consummate professional. Charlie performed impeccably, and the director was delighted. A week later, the piece went out on national television.

What happened next I could never have expected in a month of Sundays.

In the middle of the morning after the transmission I received a phone call from a secretary in the Tomorrow's World production office at the BBC. She said that they were receiving a steady stream of phone enquiries about Charlie Pluckett from people who had seen it on their programme the previous evening, and would it be OK for her to give them my phone number so that they could speak directly to me. Rather naively I said "yes".

And then the phone started ringing. Call after call. Hour after hour.

Some were from weirdos, some from robotic enthusiasts, some were from academia, and some from industry. All wanted to come and see Charlie Pluckett. One very well-respected manufacturer of industrial plastics said they needed to develop a robot to test their incontinence-wear products to see if they developed leaks. Another was a security firm that wanted animated dummy security guards to place in premises, to give would-be thieves the impression that they were being genuinely guarded by real humans.

But one of the calls was rather intriguing. The voice on the phone introduced himself as Ian Hanson, but said he wasn't in a position to divulge the name of the company he represented. All he would say was that his company had been manufacturing static dummy human figures for nearly 200 years, and the time had come to make them move. How fascinating. So I arranged an appointment when he and some of his colleagues could come to my flat for a performance.

The delegation came up from London to Cardiff on the train, changed onto the Barry Island branch line, and trudged through a rather sad-looking closed-up amusement park in the middle of winter to get to my flat. If I had known then what I know now, I would have gladly met this incredibly high-powered and influential group of people in a chauffeur-driven Rolls Royce at Cardiff Station! But minutes before they were due to arrive disaster struck. One of Charlie's glass eyeballs came un-superglued from the miniature brass pedestal inside the head on which it articulated. Instead of falling out, it fell inwards and disappeared into the mass of levers, springs and tiny cylinders in the head. There was nothing for it but to remove the rubber face mask, dismantle the head, find the eyeball and superglue it back in place. From my window I could see the train from Cardiff pulling into Barry Island railway station. "Don't panic, John!" I thought. "Keep calm"

I had just finished reassembling Charlie's head when the doorbell rang. Standing on the doorstep were four very smart-suited gentlemen. They turned out to be the Chief Executive of Madame Tussauds in London, Michael Herbert, along with two senior board directors and Ian Hanson, head of Madame Tussauds Studios. Here were the most influential people from the world's most prestigious waxworks! Goodness knows what they thought they had come to. (In later years, I would find out, and their first impressions weren't good!). But fortunately Charlie Pluckett did impress. He performed well, his eyes stayed in their sockets, and the small audience looked intrigued. They were very keen to impress upon me that, just as I wanted to keep my technology secret, they too didn't want anyone to know that they were exploring the possibility of animated figures. I agreed that I would not tell anyone that the meeting had taken place.

"How does he work?" asked Ian Hanson. "Very well indeed," was my reply. Everyone laughed politely at this vain attempt at humour on my part. But I went on to explain that I was not in a position to divulge the figure's workings. Michael Herbert then asked if I could give them a very rough idea of what a typical figure might cost, since he knew that Disney's animated figures cost many tens of thousands of dollars each. I explained that my technology was relatively simple and very cheap. Charlie performed a few more songs, I handed out cracked mugs of instant coffee and Jaffa Cakes, and they went away apparently very happy. No sooner had I closed the door behind them than I heard a crack and tinkling sound come from the room. Charlie's glass eyeball had fallen outwards this time, and was lying smashed on the floor.

Ian Hanson contacted me a few days later. He thanked me for demonstrating Charlie Pluckett, and said that Madame Tussauds were very serious indeed about meeting me to talk about taking things on to the next stage. I said I'd be happy to go to London to meet them. Once again, he stressed the need for confidentiality.

It was agreed that I'd meet Ian at Madame Tussauds Waxworks in Baker Street the following week. (I soon discovered that the word "waxworks" is strictly taboo within their company – it must be called an "exhibition of wax portraiture".)

The more I thought about it, the more this seemed to be the solution to my problem of not losing control of the simple technology I had developed. The moment I sold a figure, the secret would be out and everyone would copy it. But here was a client who was keen to work with me, and keep the secret very much to themselves. If I could negotiate a contract which would tie me into the further development of the technology for a period of time, I could earn some good money whilst working with some of the finest sculptors and moulders in the world, and really perfect the art of animated figures.

Madame Tussauds occupies a very imposing building on Marylebone Road, next to Baker Street tube station in London. It is a landmark known the world over, dominated by the huge copper dome of the London Planetarium, which is part of the attraction. In those days Madame Tussauds deliberately cultivated a mystique about how their wax figures were made. The studio was located on the very top floor of the exhibition, and was guarded like Fort Knox. Nobody was allowed into the studio, not even the exhibition staff. Even the celebrities who were being "done" in wax went into a separate VIP studio, and never got to see the real heart of the operation. The processes that they used had been developed over 200 years under the utmost secrecy, and resulted in the finest and most realistic wax portraiture in the world. So I felt very honoured when Ian Hanson gave me the full guided tour of his empire. I watched the sculptors creating the clay portraits, and the moulders making plaster moulds from the clay heads and casting them in wax. In the hair insertion department, people were inserting individual strands of human hair (one hair at a time!!!!) into the softened wax scalps. Handmade glass eyes were being manufactured from close-up photos of the celebrities' own eyes. And their own in-house dentist crafted the false teeth. It was an incredible enterprise.

Secrecy was very important at Madame Tussauds, and so it was to me. We seemed ideal partners.

Lunch had been arranged downstairs in the boardroom, but before that there was just time for a quick tour of the most famous waxworks – sorry, wax exhibition - in the world. The realism and quality of the figures was stunning, but so too was the attention to detail and the imagination put into the settings in which they were displayed. No longer the rope barriers to separate the celebrity figures from their audience ... the visitors were encouraged to get up-close and personal with their heroes. There was a real sense of showmanship to the whole operation – something with which I could definitely identify.

In the boardroom, the senior management and four of the main board directors had assembled for lunch, presided over by Michael Herbert the chief executive. I was introduced to them all, and a television was set up in a corner, on which a recording of the Tomorrow's World programme was played. Ian explained that I was the inventor of the figure, and although the assembled company appeared very impressed by the way it moved, they made it abundantly clear to me that the realism of the face left much to be desired, and that Madame Tussauds could do a lot better. Of that, I had absolutely no doubt.

After lunch, I sat down with the commercial director of Madame Tussauds London, Barry Worthing-Smith, and talked business. The first thing he did was to make me sign a confidentiality agreement, which I very happily did. Then he explained their top-secret plans.

"Madame Tussauds has just signed a lease on ..." he looked furtively around to ensure nobody had sneaked into his office with us, and was overhearing the conversation, " ... a lease on Windsor and Eton Central Railway Station, and we are about to develop a new exhibition there which will recreate Queen Victoria's Diamond Jubilee Celebrations in 1897. We are fully restoring the station and royal train for this, and producing nearly one hundred new wax figures representing relevant prominent personalities of the day."

"Yes, but where do I come in?" I asked.

"The finale of the exhibition will be a theatre show which will tell the life story of Queen Victoria using the latest audio-visual techniques ... and ... now that we've found you, fully animated figures" he continued. "Will you work with us?"

My answer was in the affirmative. We thrashed out a contract, and I agreed to deliver Charlie Pluckett to Madame Tussauds the following week.

I arrived with him in the back of a van, which I parked in the loading bay in York Court at the rear of the exhibition. No sooner had I got out of the van than security guards were ushering curious staff members away. Ian Hanson arrived with a large black sheet which was draped over poor Charlie. We waited till the coast was clear, and boarded the service elevator to the fourth floor. There, a special secure room (YC47) had been prepared for Charlie's arrival. The windows had been blacked-out to ensure no spies disguised as window cleaners could look in from outside. It really was the most extraordinary cloak-and-dagger operation.

Only a very select few at Madame Tussauds had been let in on the secret of who had taken up residence in room YC47.

The reason for all this secrecy was that if, at the last minute, just before the Windsor show opened, it was decided that the animation of the figures was not up to Madame Tussauds' high standards of realism, the mechanisms would be switched off for evermore and the figures would appear in the show as if they were any other static waxworks. And nobody would be any the wiser.

I set up Charlie with his control system, and "those in the know" (a very select group consisting of the people who'd already seen him, together with Malcolm Clarke who was Head of Audio Visual, and Ron Feakes, Studio Manager) were admitted for his performance. Even the keyhole of the door had been taped over with gaffer tape. Charlie gave a charming rendition of Peter Skellern's version of 'Love Is The Sweetest Thing' and got a standing ovation (well, nobody in the room was sitting anyway). "Are you all happy with what you've seen?" I asked. "Yes" everybody enthusiastically replied.

I was naturally apprehensive about how this august group of people would react when they saw the simplicity (and crudeness) of Charlie Pluckett's workings, and now the time had come to reveal them for the very first time. It was a most liberating experience for me, as for the previous two years I was the only person in the world privy to his technology, and at last I could reveal it to others. I removed his wig, face-mask, shirt and trousers, then took off the fibreglass shells that formed the shape of his body. What met everybody's eyes reduced them to stunned silence. They realised they had paid me thousands of pounds for a load of door hinges, bits of plywood, copper pipe, knicker elastic, some pieces of bent coat hanger and a few pneumatic cylinders. For a moment nobody said a word, and I thought I was about to become one of the exhibits in the torture chamber in the Chamber of Horrors downstairs in the basement.

But then Malcolm Clarke came to my rescue. "That's extraordinary. I can see now how you produce the amazingly smooth movement". The secret that I had developed involved using opposing springs to bias each axis of movement towards its midpoint, and then using the pneumatic cylinder to offset it from this midpoint towards its limit of travel. The closer it got to this limit, the more opposing force the springs generated, and the movement progressed to a smooth halt. Everyone then started to agree that it was the basic principals that they had bought, and that if I could make the figure work reliably and realistically using the crude materials I had employed, then with some precision engineering and their sculpting and moulding expertise we could produce something quite remarkable.

A small engineering company in Southall was engaged to do the work (again, having had to sign confidentiality agreements and set up a secure workshop) and over the next two years, Charles Dickens, Prince Albert, Benjamin Disraeli, two Queen Victorias (one young and one old), various other contemporary figures, the narrator in the likeness of the actor Frank Finlay, and a dog were all turned into fully animated figures.

The crude mechanisms within the bowels (literally) of Charlie Pluckett had been refined into beautiful pieces of precision engineering.

The Exhibition was to be called "Royalty and Empire" and the show itself was entitled "Sixty Glorious Years". The finale of the show was proving a challenge. The aged Queen Victoria had to rise from her throne, stand and give a very moving speech, sit back down again, then die. It was obvious that to do this was going to be very complicated. The way a person has to shift their weight onto the balls of their feet by leaning forward, and then keep their balance as they rise is a very tricky thing to do (or it is, at least, if you're a robot). Fortunately, the Queen was wearing a voluminous dress, and the throne was quite large, so we were able to conceal the rather cumbersome mechanism beneath the chair.

At an earlier point in the show, Ian Hanson (who was the show's director) wanted Benjamin Disraeli, the Prime Minister, to exhibit his well-documented annoying habit of nervously wiping his nose with his handkerchief when in the presence of the Queen. This meant that the figure had to raise his hand accurately to his nose, and on numerous occasions his rubber index finger would get stuck up his left nostril, and the finger would eventually free itself with a loud "plop". (This exhibition of cyber nose-picking did not amuse Her Majesty.)

Ian and I were getting on and working together very well, and when it became apparent that our animation technology could not deliver a particular realistic gesture that the script demanded from a figure (as in the aforementioned example), Ian always took a positive and flexible approach to helping me find an alternative. When this could not be done, I used the magician's tactic of diverting the audience's focus of attention away from the less-than-perfect movement towards the Queen's dog, who was curled up at her feet. Whenever a jerky or unrealistic movement occurred, just before this I would program the little mutt to yawn or wag its tail. Everybody would look towards it, and miss the offending gesture.

Eventually the show was complete and ready for its opening night. And then the DAY of JUDGEMENT came!

The entire board of Madame Tussauds, together with its Chairman, Lord Blakenham, and a newly appointed Head of Marketing, Mike Jolly, came to see a preview of the finished show. At the end, rather like a gladiatorial judgement, the show would be given either the thumbs-up or the thumbs down signal by the panel of judges.

Disraeli wiped his nose perfectly, the dog wagged its tail and yawned and Queen Victoria passed away peacefully. Ian and I turned towards the rear of the theatre and waited anxiously. Some sort of vote seemed to be taking place. The result? A unanimous thumbs up!

The exhibition opened, and the crowds flocked to see it.

Then, a very important looking envelope arrived on my doormat. Inside, the card read:

The Directors of Madame Tussauds Ltd.

have pleasure in inviting
Mr. John Wardley
to celebrate the visit of
H.M. The Queen
H.R.H. The Duke of Edinburgh
H.H. The Amir of the State of Bahrain
to the Royalty and Empire Exhibition
Windsor and Eton Central Railway Station
10.00 a.m. Wednesday 11th. April 1984

A yellow post-it note was stuck on the invitation, and in Ian Hanson's immaculate handwritten script, was written:

"You're going to meet the Queen! I'm escorting the Royal party round the exhibition with Lord Blakenham, and you're going to take them into the theatre show. Start practicing your bow!"

So I did. I was given a briefing document that is issued by the Lord Chamberlain's office of the "do's and don'ts" when meeting the Queen. (For example, you never ask the Queen to do anything. You precede any instruction with the words "If it please your Majesty..."). There were four pages of these protocols, but they all seemed very sensible and showed proper courtesy anyway.

On the great day, I was positioned outside the doors of the theatre along with Reg Gadney who had written the script of the show. After what seemed an eternity, with much cheering going on from the crowds outside, the Royal party approached. Lord Blakenham was with the Queen. Ian Hanson escorted the Duke of Edinburgh. And Michael Herbert was with the Amir of Bahrain. And they were walking straight towards Reg and me!

"May I present Mr. John Wardley, your Majesty. He has made our figures move!"

I bowed, and found myself looking straight down at the Queen's calves and ankles. They were very nice, ordinary calves and ankles. Not the sort of special calves and ankles you think a Queen should have. But then, what sort should she have?

The Queen offered her hand, which I gently shook (you don't wring the Queen's hand in a wrestler's handshake).

"Oh how very clever of you" said the Queen. "I look forward to seeing this." Then up came the Duke of Edinburgh, who really seemed to be enjoying himself, and after shaking my hand said in a somewhat abrupt but quite pleasant way "You made the things move? Sort of puppets, hmm? What will they think of next."

After the Amir was introduced, I said my well-rehearsed line to the Queen, "If it please Your Majesty, we would be honoured if you'd care to enter our theatre to see a performance of the show Sixty Glorious Years". It obviously did please Her Majesty, because in we all went.

Once the Royal Party were seated in their row, (The Queen, the D of E, the Amir and their three escorts) and myself, Reg, and two of the other Tussauds directors in the row behind, the theatre doors closed, and something extraordinary happened. The Queen's demeanor and body language changed completely. She was now behind closed doors, out of sight of the public, security guards and prying cameras. There were just ten of us in the otherwise empty theatre. She was obviously enjoying herself (the whole theme of the exhibition was about one of her ancestors, after all) and she relaxed. More than that, you felt she was genuinely interested in the comfort and welfare of not just her guest, the Amir of Bahrain, but all of us in that theatre.

As the show started and Charles Dickens recited a passage from one of his novels, the Queen looked over her shoulder at me and smiled. When Disraeli blew his nose, the Duke was heard to mutter "Bloody clever!" I was warned in advance that "The Queen does not applaud". But at the end of the show, the Queen did give a dignified applaude of appreciation. And I thought "Little does Her Majesty realise that she is applauding a load of rubber, pneumatic cylinders, levers and springs".

Once outside the theatre, the Queen's regal presence returned, and the procession moved along the station concourse. Every minute detail of the building had been faithfully restored to its former glory, including the booking hall, and the ladies and gents toilets. Considerable effort had gone into finding exact replicas of the sanitaryware and plumbing that would have been installed in Victorian public loos of the time.

As the party was about to pass the gents toilet, I could see that Ian and the Duke of Edinburgh were engaged in some animated banter, and suddenly the two of them peeled off from the group and marched into the gents! Ian was keen to show the Duke his restoration efforts. As he entered the door, Ian turned to me and very firmly beckoned me to follow. By the time I was inside, the Duke of Edinburgh was standing at the urinal, and making use of its welcome facility. Ian was stood on one side of him, and he beckoned me to stand at the other. I can now say that I've pee'd with Royalty.

The three of us emerged to find that the Queen and the rest of the Royal Party were standing outside waiting for us to come out, and Her Majesty was looking rather bemused. I don't suppose the Queen has ever stood outside a public loo before (or since) waiting for anyone to come out! Goodbyes were said by all, and they then boarded their limousine and headed off back to Windsor Castle up the hill. I could just imagine the Queen sitting in the back of her limo saying to the Duke and the Amir "Fancy a quiet night in, boys. Phillip can pop out and get a Chinese, and we can eat it and watch Corrie".

But perhaps the ultimate accolade that Madame Tussauds can bestow on anybody is to "do" them in wax, and that's exactly what happened to me. At the entrance to the exhibition for all to see was the Royal Coach, and who should be mounted on horseback as postillion driving the coach? Me!

I'm introduced to Her Majesty the Queen
at the official opening of "Royalty & Empire" exhibition

I meet myself in wax

Chapter 11

THE WONDERFUL WORLD OF ADVENTURES

Let's turn the clock back 12 months.

Whilst in the middle of building the figures for Windsor's Royalty and Empire exhibition, I bumped into Graham Jackson, one of the directors of Madame Tussauds, in a corridor in the York Court offices. The company's portfolio of attractions at that time consisted of Madame Tussauds wax exhibitions in London and Amsterdam, together with Wookey Hole Caves in Somerset, Warwick Castle, and Chessington Zoo. Graham was the director responsible for Chessington.

Chessington Zoo was ideally located just to the South of London, very close to the route of the proposed new M25 motorway. But it was having a hard time. Visitor numbers were dropping alarmingly, and Graham was charged with the responsibility of turning its fortunes around. He said that he understood that I knew something about fairground rides and shows, and asked if I could go to Chessington to "sort out the funfair and the circus" (these were his very words). I said I'd be pleased to take a look, and one Friday I arranged to meet him there.

We had a walk around, and what I found was a nice little zoo (if rather unimaginatively presented), a very ordinary tented circus show, and a rather tatty travelling funfair. As we sat in the audience to watch the circus show, some space-age music started and into the ring trundled a flying saucer. "I've seen that somewhere before!" I thought. Yes, it was the same aerial act I'd helped with way back in my days at the Yarmouth Hippodrome. They were now the stars of the show (and the best act, by far!).

The management team gave me a very nice lunch in their boardroom, we exchanged lots of pleasantries and platitudes, and I departed saying I'd give it some thought and report back. My time was very pre-occupied with the Windsor show, and I felt that Chessington's fortunes could not be turned around by replacing some tatty fairground rides with some slightly better fairground rides, or replacing a mediocre circus show with a somewhat better circus show. So I wrote Graham

Jackson a letter, saying I did not think the answer to Chessington's problems lay in "sorting out the funfair and the circus".

He sent me a very nice letter in reply, which basically said "Thank you very much, but don't call us, we'll call you." And I thought that was the end of the matter.

But 12 months later after Royalty and Empire had opened, I received a phone call.

"You won't know me, but my name's Ray Barratt, and I'm the new director of Madame Tussauds responsible for Chessington Zoo. I've been looking through my predecessor's files, and I've found a rather enigmatic letter from you, saying that you "do not think the answer to Chessington's problems lay in *sorting out the funfair and the circus.*". Reading between the lines, can I take it that you do think you have an answer to its problems? If so, we ought to meet!"

This was the phonecall from heaven!

Ray Barratt turned out to be one of the most inspirational people I've ever met. He had an accountancy background, and experience in developing and running safari parks and tourist attractions around the world. Although he was the first person to admit he wasn't especially creative himself, he knew how to recognise that talent in other people. He had a knack of pulling together teams of experts in their fields, letting them do their job without unnecessary interference, and leading those teams forward to bring projects to fruition.

After Royalty and Empire opened, I had some time on my hands. Incognito, I snuck into Chessington Zoo and had a good walk around. Slowly, a plan started to form in my mind.

One of the problems the big American theme park companies had in getting an attraction off the ground in Britain (and the reason it had not happened up to this point) was the enormous cost of infrastructure to get a site secure, landscaped, and all the services and facilities needed behind the scenes developed. And that was before they had even started to consider the cost of the rides and entertainments within. At Chessington, all that was already on site. If we could weave themed rides around the animal exhibits, and have a pay-one-price policy for admission, this could be an economically-viable way of creating Britain's first true theme park.

At this point, let me pontificate on what I think a "theme park" is.

For some reason, people have come to believe that a theme park is any kind of clean-cut fairground, preferably on an inland site, with a few trees and rose-bushes planted between the rides, and a pay-one-price admission policy (in other words, you pay to go in, then everything inside is free.) Perhaps the rides are given exotic sounding names (e.g. a logflume called "Zambezi Falls", or a rollercoaster named "The Python") and embellished with suitably designed signs, but that is as far as the "theming" goes.

This is simply not the case!

That is not what a proper theme park is.

A true theme park uses the same techniques I worked with in the film industry – highly realistic film-set scenery and special effects, together with characters and stories to produce a show. The only difference is that instead of the audience sitting in a cinema or theatre to watch the show, they are actually part of it. So although Alton Towers at that point in time was calling itself a theme park, it wasn't. It simply had large fairground rides which were notionally decorated, nicely landscaped, and they charged one admission price. Alton Towers wasn't a proper theme park in my definition of the phrase. (It was soon to change ... I made sure of that ... but we'll come on to that later!)

I was convinced that the commercially-viable way to turn Chessington Zoo into Britain's first true theme park was to conceal beneath the veneer of the fantasy environment some conventional amusement park hardware, but to ensure that it was buried so deep amongst the scenery and special effects that it had no more prominence within the entertainment experience than your seat in a theatre or cinema. The rides would be used as nothing more than a way to get the audience through the show. The ride hardware would not be the show itself. And this is the fundamental difference between a Theme Park and an Amusement Park.

So as I walked around the zoo, I visualised exotically-themed lands ... The Mystic East, the Wild West, and so on. In the Wild West would be a runaway goldmine train ... only bigger, better and faster than the Whacky Goldmine I'd built at Barry Island. Its mode of transport would actually be a rollercoaster, but that's not what the visitors would think about as they whizzed through the tunnels. In the Mystic East I could visualise an exciting river journey past temples and pagodas, and down waterfalls. Yes, it would have at its heart conventional logflume technology, but that wasn't what the riders would see.

By the time I'd left Chessington Zoo my mind was buzzing with excitement. I knew that one of the first questions Ray Barratt was going to ask me when I talked through my ideas was "How much is it going to cost?" So I contacted ride manufacturers, scenic construction and civil engineering companies and started to get a rough handle on budgets. Then I put my proposals to him in his office at Madame Tussauds. Halfway through the meeting, Michael Herbert the Chief Executive (who'd heard that I was in the building) popped his head round Ray's office door to say hello. "What are you doing here?" Michael asked. "Ray's asked me to come up with some ideas for Chessington," I replied.

Without saying a word, he came into the office and sat down, listening intently to what I was saying. After a few minutes he said "Stop right there!"

"Oh no," I thought. "That's the end of that!"

But he picked up the phone on Ray's desk, and said "Harry, come into Ray's office if you have a moment". A minute later, in walked Harry Streets, another of the main board directors. Harry and I talked the same language, as his family had been prominent manufacturers of coin-operated amusement machines for years, and he operated amusement arcades at the south coast seaside resort of Worthing.

"Have a listen to this, Harry," said Michael as he joined our group.

After I'd finished my presentation, Ray said "What do you think, chaps?"

"Sounds interesting," said Harry "but what's it going to cost?"

Fortunately, I was prepared, and pulled out of my briefcase a wad of papers with breakdowns of typical costs which my good friend John Collins at Barry Island had helped me prepare, using the experience we had in building the logflume there a few years previously. Harry noticed that some of these notes were written in someone else's hand on Barry Island Pleasure Park headed notepaper.

"Is John Collins involved in this?" Harry asked.

I explained that I had done a lot of work for John and his brother Pat at Barry Island, and John had indeed helped to finance the original development of Charlie Pluckett. It turned out that Harry knew John through the Amusement Caterer's Association, and they had a great deal of mutual respect.

The meeting had gone well, and the directors decided that I would be given the task of devising a masterplan for the re-vitalisation of Chessington Zoo. Ray Barratt, being the skilled manager that he was, realised that in addition to me, he needed to pull a team of people together who could contribute the other specialist skills required to design and fully-cost a set of proposals. It was agreed that John Collins would be asked to be part of that team.

Before I left his office, Ray pulled out of a filing cabinet a folder containing details of an approach which had recently been made to Madame Tussauds to invest in a Watership Down theme park development near Newbury in Berkshire. "Fancy a trip down the M4 to take a look at this? It might give us some ideas," he said.

We arranged a date, and a few weeks later we attended a presentation in a barn on the proposed site. The proposals were brilliantly presented by a very personable landscape architect who entranced us with his visuals and plans, but the project itself was seriously flawed. "The project's not for us, but the guy behind the presentation's a genius. We need him on our team!" we both agreed. His name was Andy Nichols, and he did indeed join our team as landscape architect and planner.

Ray had worked for many years with a civil engineer called Peter Barber who knew all about concrete, and sewers, and electricity supplies, and things like that. He completed the team.

Gradually, as things progressed, it became apparent that the biggest hurdle to overcome was not technical or financial, but local authority Planning Legislation. The Royal Borough of Kingston upon Thames was not going to let us do just what we wanted, and put enormous obstacles in our paths. They would not allow us to develop anything that could be seen or heard from outside the site, and the peace and tranquility of the zoo exhibits would have to be maintained so as not to disturb the animals.

But eventually a scheme was agreed, and Pearson's, the owners of Madame Tussauds, gave the project the go-ahead. The Pearson Group were a huge multi-national conglomerate whose core business at that time was publishing. They owned Penguin Books, the Financial Times, Pearson Longman etc. But they also had an assortment of companies in unrelated fields including Chateau Latour Wine, Royal Doulton China ... and Madame Tussauds. In addition they just happened to own Lazards the investment bankers. So they weren't short of a few bob to invest in Chessington, as long as it gave them a good return.

In addition to the team Ray Barratt had lined up for the project, I added Mike Blackman from Chichester (remember him? He built Uncle Frankenstein for the Scream Machine) to be in charge of scenic construction. The ride hardware was ordered, and work on site started. Mike Jolly was group head of marketing, and he appointed a marketing manager to the project. After long and involved discussions it was decided that the new attraction was going to be called:

Chessington World of Adventures

In the first phase of development, a monorail would be built around the site to give the visitors a preview of the new attraction as it was being constructed. And then the following year, 1987, the completed theme park would open. This comprised of a Runaway Train, a heavily themed water-ride and a dark ride, all built by the German ride manufacturer Heinrich Mack. The circus area would be transformed into Circus World, with a participation circus academy and various sideshows to support the main circus show. A number of smaller rides and attractions were to be interspersed amongst the main rides, and the whole park re-landscaped.

Up to this point in the project, Madame Tussauds Studios had nothing to do with the development (I believe that secretly they thought funfairs and circuses were a bit beneath them. They were artists, after all!) but the idea of a dark ride with animated figures and a storyline really appealed to Ian Hanson, and he took responsibility for this aspect of the project. I designed a novel transit system for him, whereby the trains of vehicles could stop at various places along the route, and the cars all turn to face one direction to allow the "audience" to watch each of the animated scenes as the story unfolded. Ian commissioned Douglas Adams (the writer of Hitchhiker's Guide to the Galaxy) to write the story and script, and Richard Hartley composed and recorded the music.

The team Ray Barratt had assembled to develop Chessington World of Adventures worked well together. We each had our own clear roles and areas of expertise. I was responsible for the design of the rides and entertainments, Andy Nichols for the landscaping and visual environment, Peter Barber for the construction, and John Collins for the operational management.

The park opened for Easter 1987, and immediately it was obvious to us all that we had achieved our objective of turning around the fortunes of the old Chessington Zoo. Chessington World of Adventures was a resounding success.

The official opening was to be conducted by His Royal Highness Prince Edward on Monday July 6th. 1987.

I was told that after I had been introduced to him, my main role was to ask HRH if he'd like to take a ride on the Dragon River Water ride. As I was nervously waiting at my allocated position at the entrance to the ride for the Royal party to arrive, I was trying to remember what I'd be told when I'd met the Queen about what you mustn't say when asking a member of the Royal Family to do something. "If it please your Royal Highness …". Yes, that was the phrase. I repeated my line over and over again. "If it please your Royal Highness, would you care to take a ride on our Dragon River attraction, sir?"

I was still repeating this under my breath as he approached me. He was introduced to me by Nigel Martin, the park's General Manager, and Prince Edward immediately started chatting away to me in a most friendly and informal way. I was so caught off my guard I blurted out to him, "Fancy a ride on the logflume?" "Oh, yes that'd be great. I've never been on one of those before."

With HRH Prince Edward at the official opening
of Chessington World of Adventures

A grand official luncheon took place afterwards in a marquee that had been set up on the front lawn of Burnt Stub Mansion at the centre of the park. As well as His Royal Highness, local dignitaries and company executives, various prominent members of the amusement park industry had been invited. I found myself sitting next to Geoffrey Thompson who was managing director of Blackpool Pleasure Beach. I had met him on numerous occasions before, and admired his park enormously. He had pioneered many novel and unusual attractions at the Pleasure Beach, and shared my view that travelling fairground rides belonged just there … in travelling fairgrounds, not in permanent amusement parks, let alone *theme* parks!

We were so engrossed in conversation that we were oblivious of the other guests on our table. "Now that you've opened this new park, what plans have you got for the future?" Geoffrey asked. I explained that I was still not very enamoured by the circus show that was being presented in the Circus World area of the park, and had plans to replace it with a big spectacular magic show. He asked me if I knew anything about magic, and I told him about my background, but explained that this new show might not happen for quite a few years ahead.

He explained that in one of his Blackpool cabaret theatres called the Horseshoe Showbar, he had presented a spectacular variety show for many years. The first year it was "Viva Las Vegas!", the second year "Viva Paris!", then "Viva Brazil!" and so on. But now after 12 years they were beginning to run out of new Viva ideas (I believe the current one was "Viva Basingstoke!" or something). He asked if I'd be interested in working with him and his show producer to come up with a new show format based on magic and illusions.

I checked with Ray Barratt to make sure this wouldn't present a conflict of interests, and he said, if anything, it might be to our benefit for the future.

So I went up to Blackpool, and met with Geoffrey and Gloria Gee (known to everyone as Glo), his show producer. She had produced the Pleasure Beach's world-renowned ice shows and cabarets for many years, and was an immensely talented lady who knew her craft inside out. As with my experiences at Great Yarmouth, when the "boss" brings a mate of his in as an apparent "expert" onto an established team, one had to be sensitive to people's feelings. Fortunately, Glo had no such insecurities, and very soon realised I was a useful person to have around. We got on like a house on fire. We discussed the overall format of the show, which was to have a slightly edgy gothic feel to it, and considered various illusions that could be presented on suitable themes, and have dance numbers woven around them.

Soon we had a basic outline drafted, which Geoffrey Thompson approved, and I started work to track down manufacturers of the illusions. Magicians were auditioned for the main lead part, along with a supporting company of dancers, singers, a speciality act, and a comedian. One of the illusions required compressed air to operate it, so we installed a powerful air compressor on the roof of the Casino complex which housed the Horseshoe Bar. One lunchtime, the three of us escaped from the confines of Blackpool to have a bite of lunch in a little country pub called the "Hand and Dagger" at nearby Kirkham. "What are we going to called this show?" Geoffrey asked. Various ideas were thrown around, many of which were unbelievably silly, until I came up with the name 'Mystique'. And that's what the show was called.

When the rehearsal period arrived, Geoffrey Thompson very kindly gave me the use of the family's beautiful penthouse flat in the Casino building which they kept for their personal use and that of their friends and visitors. It was decorated in art deco style, with original fittings and decoration from when the complex was first built in 1937 by Joseph Emberton. It was an incredibly hot night, with not a breath of wind in the air (very unusual for Blackpool's bracing Golden Mile!) and I was lying in bed at 2 o'clock in the morning unable to sleep with the heat, with not a stitch of clothing on. Then I discovered something else was keeping me awake. I'd forgotten to switch off the air compressor on the roof immediately outside the penthouse flat, and its noise was disturbing my slumber. There was nothing for it but to go out of the fire escape door, onto the roof and switch it off.

This I duly did, but on returning to the door I discovered it had slammed shut, and there was no way of opening it from the outside. I was trapped on the roof of the building stark naked. But there was a way out. Also on top of the building was the Attic Disco and Nightclub, and its fire escape door had been left open because of the heat. With all the courage I could muster I crept across the roof to the door to the nightclub full of revelers. I took a deep breath and ran in. I streaked through the packed club much to the amazement of some and the encouraging cheers of others. I made a bee-line for the privacy of the elevator. I ran in, the doors closed, and I relaxed. But my respite was very short lived, when I discovered that it was a glasselevator that ran down the outside of the façade of the building facing the Golden Mile. My naked descent was very public.

The finale of the show was a very ambitious illusion, where the entire cast would take their individual bows, and then ascend a short flight of steps to enter a small curtained booth raised up above the apron stage in the middle of the auditorium, so that the audience could see underneath and all around it. After the company of 15 performers had entered the booth, the star of the show would come on, take his bow, go into the booth, and instantly there would be a loud bang and flash, and the curtains would drop to reveal the booth completely empty. At the same time the cast would appear amongst the audience with bottles of champagne, giving out glasses of bubbly to the dumbfounded spectators.

Now, I bet you're wondering how we did this. Well, whenever a lay-person finds out how a baffling illusion is accomplished, either by being told, or using surreptitious methods, they invariably feel a sense of disappointment. The magic and wonder goes, and the whole thing becomes mundane. They also think, "That wouldn't fool anybody!".

So when the cast were about to be taught how to do this finale illusion (which they had never seen before) I was determined that they should first experience it as the audience would see it. I wanted them to be amazed and in awe of it. I went around the Pleasure Beach offices and recruited an assortment of secretaries, cashiers, waiters and kitchen staff, and that evening when the show's cast had gone home from rehearsals, I taught this motley crew how to perform the illusion. The following day I sat the cast in the auditorium, and our new amateur recruits performed the illusion for them. The cast were amazed. They couldn't believe their eyes.

How on earth was it done? Where did they vanish to? They couldn't wait to find out.

And then I showed them the secret. And a cloud seemed to descend on their enthusiasm. "That's not going to fool anybody," one was heard to mutter. But, as it turned out, it did fool a lot of people, nearly 160,000 people during the many years the show ran. So next time you yearn to find out how a trick is done, remember you have a wonderful advantage over the magician who is performing it. Because to you it is amazing, fantastic, incredible. To the magician its just a trick. Let's keep it that way.

One of the illusions we created for "Mystique"

Chapter 12

VAMPIRES AND BUBBLES

By mid-summer of 1987 it was apparent that Chessington World of Adventures' first season was going far better than we had dared hope, and in recognition of this I was made a director of a new company called Tussauds Group Park Developments Ltd. My first task in this role was to put my thinking cap on and start planning for the next phase of Chessington's development, and get ideas for new rides and attractions. The time it took to negotiate with the local authority planners for planning consent in the first phase indicated to us that we had to start serious negotiations with them straight away if we had any hope of opening some new and exciting rides in 1990.

But let's take a little side trip away from Chessington for a moment.

One day I received a phone call from the Chief Executive of the Wales Tourist Board for whom I had still been doing occasional consultancy work.

"John, we're in a spot of bother. A family of potato farmers in West Wales have put in an application for grant-aid to develop a theme park in Pembrokeshire. It's obviously a non-starter, as they don't know the first thing about theme parks and they've got a pitifully small budget, but we've been a bit tardy in responding to them, and they've complained to the Welsh Office that we're not doing our job. Be a good chap, pop down there to see them, then write an official report saying the project's a non-starter and that the WTB shouldn't help finance it. And that will get them off our backs."

Well, that was not a very open brief! However, I agreed to go down and see them.

The McNamara family consisted of Mum (Delphine), Dad (Geoff), their sons (William and Paddy), and their daughter (Fran), together with wives, husbands, and numerous grandchildren. As soon as I met them it became apparent that (a) true, they didn't know much about theme parks, but (b) they had a great sense of family fun, (c) they had an amazing site, ideal for development of a theme park and (d) it was close to the thousands of holidaymakers that stayed along the Pembrokeshire coast during the summer. Agreed, they didn't have the multi-million dollar budgets the big American parks had, but that shouldn't stop the project being viable.

I had a wonderful day with them all, and felt that their site and its location would make an ideal theme park, and the McNamara family, with a bit of help, were potentially well-suited to developing and operating it. So I decided that I would not write the report in the way I'd been asked to write it. Instead, I said that I thought that the project should be supported by the Wales Tourist Board and that if Wales was ever to get its own major theme park, this was the one. As you can imagine, this did not go down at all well with the WTB, and I've not been asked to do a day's work for them since! But it had a very happy outcome indeed. As a consequence of my report (which went on record), the Wales Tourist Board were forced to provide the family with financial grant-aid, and I acted as a consultant to the project. Oakwood Theme Park became a reality, and I've been associated with it ever since.

I hope you enjoyed that little excursion into Wales. Now let's get back to Chessington.

The rides that we'd developed in phase one were nice middle-of-the-road family attractions. The Runaway Train was fast, but not too scary. But a lot of visitor feedback was saying "We want a really thrilling rollercoaster!"

Rollercoasters tend to be big, tall things, which loom up on the horizon and make their presence felt for miles around. The Royal Borough of Kingston upon Thames, and its residents, would not be happy about that. So we had to be somewhat clever. I looked around the park. Obviously the highest parts of the site were where the coaster would be most visible, and the lowest where it could be hidden from view. The existing Bird Garden near the bottom of the site looked as if it needed a good overhaul. If the birds and their aviaries were relocated to a different part of the zoo, and became a new themed area constructed in a higher-quality and more imaginative way, this would free-up a large part of the site for the development of the new ride.

But what sort of rollercoaster? Because we couldn't rely on height, it would have to be something that didn't rely on tall vertiginous drops to provide thrills for its riders. The well-respected American ride manufacturer, Arrow Dynamics, had produced a novel rollercoaster where the cars were suspended beneath the track and swung freely like pendulums when going round bends. I went out to the States and visited this ride, called the 'Big Bad Wolf' at Busch Gardens in Williamsburg, Virginia. It was splendid, and just what I thought Chessington needed. But since the whole ethos of Chessington World of Adventures was to set the rides in appropriately-theme "lands", we needed to come up with a theme for a whole new area for the park, and ensure the ride hardware became nothing more than a transit system for the theatricality and drama we wanted the visitors to experience within the theme.

The characteristics of the ride suggested flight. But although the ride was to be located in the old bird garden, I felt something more dramatic than birds was needed ... What about bats? *Vampire bats*! ... TRANSYLVANIA!

We'd got it!

But in addition to the rollercoaster, we wanted to create a family-friendly dark ride. Something crazy and fun, that everyone could go on and enjoy. I had in my mind's eye that our version of Transylvania would be a cute mid-European town with pretty Bavarian architecture. (Yes, I know Transylvania is in Romania, but we're a theme park, dammit!). And every Bavarian town has its Oompah Band playing in the town square outside its Hofbrauhaus brewery. Obviously alcoholic beverages aren't family-friendly, but what if our brewery made soda-pop? And our guests would be taken on a tour of this factory floating along in little barrels through each of the various departments ... the juice extracting department, the fizzy gas mixing department, the bottling department ...   It would be colourful, musical, crazy and happy!

Not many people know this, but Cardiff was home to a huge animated cartoon production industry. The main Hollywood Studios farmed-out a lot of cartoon production work to one Cardiff-based studio in particular, Siriol Productions, and their main storyboard and gag-writer was a guy called Andrew Offiler, whom I knew. He agreed to meet me, I explained my idea, and immediately his pen started sketching across the page (... Where do you make orange squash? In an orange Squash Court, of course! How do you make ginger beer? You squeeze a packet of Ginger Nut biscuits! How do you make cream soda? You blow up a cow with fizzy gas, and give it a good squeeze!). The ideas were coming non-stop from Andrew's brilliant mind and pen.

Soon, a complete illustrated storyboard was produced, packed full of whacky gags and crazy characters. The star of the show would be the owner of the factory Professor Burp, his assistants would be the Burp Boffins and the workers would be the Bubbleheads. And we named the ride 'Professor Burp's Bubbleworks'.

But who could we get to build it? The answer was very obvious ... Sparky!

Keith Sparkes was one of the amusement industry's characters. His company, Sparkes Creative Services, had produced rides and walk-through shows (particularly Haunted Houses) for amusement parks all over the country. Although it sounded like a big company, it only consisted of three people ... Keith, his business partner Kevin Finn, and their long-suffering secretary Kathleen. The secret to the company's success was that Keith had built up a network of skilled freelance out-workers based in the vicinity of Sparkes' office near Colchester in Essex. When times were hard, there were just the three of them on the payroll. But when things got busy, a huge team of talented people could be pulled together at short notice to produce some amazingly fast results.

Keith was a larger-than-life personality. He came from a family of undertakers (!) but Keith had become a puppeteer, before moving on to specialising in animated shop-window displays and Father Christmas grottos. From there he progressed to amusement park displays and puppet shows.

But it was Sparky's sense of humour that we all remember. It was delightfully juvenile, and closely matched that of an eight-year-old schoolboy. Anything to do with bottoms, bosoms or farts would send him into paroxysms of helpless laughter. It wasn't the actual joke that was funny, it was the way he *told* it. Most of his jokes were filthy, but he did have one clean one. This is it:

"When I was a lad, we were so poor, we had to buy my school uniform from the Army and Navy Stores. And, believe me, it's no joke going to Station Street Infants School dressed as a Japanese Admiral"

Now, it's not the funniest joke in the world by any means, but when Sparky told it, it became hilarious; by the time he'd got to "*we were so poor*" he'd started to giggle. By "*And believe me*" he was in fits of laughter. After "*Station Street Infants School*" his face had become bright red and the tears were running down his cheeks. On the word "*Japanese*" his eyes were bulging, incontinence was a serious issue, and paramedic attention was imminently needed. As far as I can remember, he never managed to get the word "*Admiral*" out, and it was many years later before someone else told me the punch line.

That was the joy of working with Sparky. He, and his partner Kevin came to Chessington and we went through the storyboard and the layout plans I'd drawn up for the ride. I thought Kevin's face was familiar, and it turned out that Kevin and his wife, Eve Graham, had been half of the famous pop group The New Seekers, and that Eve was the person who had tried to "Teach The World to Sing … in perfect harmony" … and sold a trillion bottles of Coca Cola as a result!

It was arranged that an initial production meeting would be held at their offices on Mersea Island near Colchester. When I arrived, a large group of people had already assembled, and I was introduced to them one by one. There was Donald Owen the sculptor, Mike Seaton the animation engineer, Bruce Carter the scenic artist, Graham Owens the audio-visual engineer … the list went on. The room was dominated by a huge scale model they had built of the ride, with every piece of scenery, prop and character reproduced down to the last detail. I had asked for a big model, as I wanted to be able to run a video camera through it so that it could be viewed from the perspective of a rider, but this was ENORMOUS! In one corner of this beautiful work of art was a nameplate of the model's maker. It said "Rex Studios", and the name "Bruce Carter". Something vaguely familiar was going through my mind.

I turned to Bruce, who spoke with a delightful Norfolk accent, and said "Have you worked for Rex Studios long?", to which he replied "Man and boy, from the age of 16. I own the company now." And then the penny dropped. Bruce was the young boy I'd met at Rex Studios in Great Yarmouth who had turned up that Sunday morning to hand over the posters to me during my fly-posting duties more than twenty years earlier. He was the one who displayed an amazing talent for air-brushing the giant portraits of the stars. And he had risen through the company to eventually own it, and become one of the main suppliers of theatrical scenery to the amusement industry. It's a small world! (now that would make a good name for a ride, wouldn't it?).

Incidentally, I recently reminisced about Sparky's jokes with Bruce, and he reminded me the other clean one he used to frequently tell: " I went to buy a bar of soap the other day. The guy said do you want it scented? I said, no, I'll take it now." It's the daft ones that are the funniest.

I wanted the Bubbleworks ride to be packed full of action, and capture the chaotic atmosphere of a really crazy factory. The use of round barrels as the vehicles would cause them to spin around as they floated along the water course. I had got this idea from my memories as a child of riding the River Caves at Margate's Dreamland amusement park. Whereas the regular boats in most water-borne dark rides proceeded at a stately pace in a forward direction, with the riders simply looking ahead, the tubs in the River Caves created a much more exciting journey as the riders' attentions were focused in every direction as they spun around, and the pace of travel seemed much faster than it actually was.

Music was going to be crucial to add to the atmosphere. I decided a specially-composed theme tune was needed, and that every area of the ride would have the same basic theme playing, but each arranged in a suitably-themed manner according to the department in the factory through which you were passing. So at the factory entrance would be an "Oompah-band" arrangement, in the Juice Extraction Room the same tune would be playing but it would have a "squishy and squidgy" arrangement, in the Fizzy Gas department it would be "hissy and bubbly", and in the Tasting & Testing department it would be "burps and farts", and so on. But this posed a huge problem, as the sound from one area would bleed into the next, and the whole thing could be a complete cacophony. This was solved by creating one gigantic multi-track soundtrack so that the entire composition was synchronised together as one musical arrangement, with the different tracks picked-off in the relevant areas. Fortunately, technology was on our side, as solid-state sound stores had just become available to enable us to do this. I selected a very talented composer, Graham Smart, and together we worked in his studio in Cardiff to compose and record what would become a very popular and catchy soundtrack.

The Vampire rollercoaster and the Bubbleworks dark ride went into construction. The great day came when the American engineers from Arrow Dynamics were due to test the Vampire, and send it round the track on its maiden voyage. As with most rollercoasters, it was a gravity ride, which meant that once the train had left the top of the lift, it literally coasted under its own momentum up and down the undulating track back to the station, with no other means of motive power. It either worked, or it didn't. Although I had every confidence that it was going to run OK (and it was being built by one of the most experienced rollercoaster manufacturers in the world), I decided that the first run would be done with the bare minimum of people hanging around watching.

So I deliberately put the rumour out that the initial test run would take place the following afternoon, whereas I'd secretly arranged with the testing engineers from Arrow that we'd assemble on site the previous midnight, and have a clandestine test run when nobody was around. It was a cold, dark, overcast moonless night when the six of us met at the Vampire station in Transylvania.

The machinery and hydraulics were run-up, and, once all the safety checks had been made, they released the brakes that were holding the train in the station. Slowly it started its maiden voyage. The Vampire was about to fly for the first time! It picked up on the chain lift that took it up to the highest point of the track, making the characteristic clicking noise as the anti-rollback ratchets operated. Then, clunk, it disengaged from the chain and started to pick up speed as it descended the first dip. Faster and faster it rolled, and louder and louder was the roaring sound it made. But in the pitch dark we could see absolutely nothing. It was out there somewhere, running out of our control! The only clue we had to its progress was its noise. We could tell it was approaching the second hill, as the roaring sound decreased, and the speed of the train dropped during its ascent. Then the roar increased again, and we knew it had crested the hill and was starting to go down into the next dip. And this went on and on, as the train went round the track.

But on one of the hills things went very quiet. Very quiet indeed. "It's stalled!" said Dale, one of the American engineers. We peered through the darkness but could see nothing. And then we heard the noise again, getting louder and louder. We all cheered. But our euphoria was short-lived, as we soon discovered that the train was running *backwards*. It had not quite made one of the hills, and instead of rolling forward over the crest it had rolled back from whence it came! It settled after several back-and-forth rolls down into the bottom of a dip. We were all devastated. The Arrow engineers got on the phone to their office back in Utah and told their boss, Ron Toomer, what had happened.

"Stalled? Our coasters never stall!" he protested. "Is the weather cold?"

"Freezing!", came Dale's reply.

"You were running with sandbags in the trains, weren't you?" queried Ron.

Whoops! They had forgotten to put weighted sandbags into the train's cars to simulate a normal payload. I would later discover that once a rollercoaster is fully run-in, it is perfectly capable of getting round the track empty and without any passengers. But for the first run in cold weather, when everything is new and the wheel-bearings are stiff, extra weight is needed to give the train added momentum.

Using a winch, the American engineers pulled the train forwards out of the dip, over the crest of the hill on which it had stalled, and it ran happily back into the station. We put sandbags onto the seats in the cars and set the train off again. It completed the circuit perfectly. The next day, half of Surrey seemed to have turned out to watch the Vampire's "maiden" (?) voyage. We feigned looking very nervous, and of course it behaved impeccably!

As well as the Vampire and the Bubbleworks, Transylvania also boasted a large food and beverage outlet called the Black Forest Chateau. This included an animated organist playing a mighty Wurlitzer cinema organ on a stage, with elaborate Bavarian décor. Live entertainment was provided around the entire area in the form of jolly vampires and oompah bands.

The 1990 season opened, and again we seemed to have got it right!

Chapter 13

THE TOWERS

After Chessington's second phase had opened, Madame Tussauds owners, Pearsons, decided that we should continue expanding. They obviously saw considerable potential for the concept we had developed.

But although Pearsons wanted us to expand, the Royal Borough of Kingston upon Thames definitely didn't! It was obvious to us all that the way forward, building bigger, better, more spectacular rides and attractions, could not be done at Chessington with the huge restrictions the local planners put on the site. So if we couldn't expand at Chessington, we'd have to look elsewhere.

We needed somewhere with (a) a nice mature landscape, (b) good access to large conurbations of people, and (c) potential planning consents to enable us to build rides, shows and attractions. Ray Barratt, Andy Nichols and I looked at many different locations. At the redundant Corby Steelworks site there was good access and local planners were falling over themselves to give out planning consents to get something developed on this brown-field site with high local unemployment. But there was no pleasant and mature landscape. At Woburn Abbey, there was beautiful landscape, good access, but no way would we get planning consent. Every site we looked at, only two of the three requirements could be met.

On several occasions I had reason to phone up colleagues at Alton Towers to discuss ride technicalities and other issues, and nearly every time the telephonist would say "I'm sorry, he's not here today, he's down at the Battersea."

John Broome, the owner of Alton Towers, was struggling to get his Battersea Power Station theme park project in London underway. Things were going badly wrong, and his bold claim that the park *"will open on 21 May 1990 at 2.30pm. Don't come at 2.35pm or you'll miss it,"* was beginning to haunt him.

It was apparent that Alton Towers was being drained of resources as a result, and things seemed to be in decline there too.

I put two-and-two together, and deduced that Alton Towers might be coming on the market, and told Ray Barratt this. Here was a ready-made park, with all the boxes ticked, just waiting for us to get our teeth into. As with the old Chessington Zoo, I made an anonymous visit to the park and had a good look around. There was enormous potential for improvement and expansion. The owners just hadn't appreciated that for every individual that actually goes on a ride, five more can be having a huge amount of fun standing and watching. A good example of this missed opportunity was the Rapids ride that they had built. It was located on a large piece of land, completely inaccessible to spectators. Unless you made the decision to go through the entrance and join the queue, you got hardly a glimpse of the adventure about to unfold. Other attractions were good, but unimaginatively presented. It just wasn't a true theme park, in my definition of the word.

I felt confident that we could use the experience we had gained in developing Chessington World of Adventures to make Alton Towers become something really special. So we bought it!

The local planning authority was Staffordshire Moorlands District Council, and one of the first things we needed to do was to establish what their attitude would be towards development at Alton Towers. Whereas Chessington had been a regular suburban site, here was a Grade II listed Augustus Pugin architectural masterpiece, set in Humphry Repton designed historic gardens, located in Staffordshire Moorlands and adjacent to the Peak District National Park. This was going to be like treading on eggshells!

Fortunately, the whole team, and in particular Andy Nichols our landscape architect, were sympathetic and fully understood the sensitivity of this situation and the fragility of the asset we had acquired. We had no intention of raping this historic gem, or ruining the beauty of its surroundings. We felt we had a responsibility not just to our owners to make them money, but also to preserve our English heritage, and make our visitors aware of it and appreciate it. It was perhaps because of this genuine attitude of ours when we approached the local Planners that they realised we were fully aware of the site's sensitivity, and they developed a positive attitude towards discussing our plans. And what were those plans?

The Madame Tussauds brand was held in great esteem worldwide, and epitomized quality and excellence. We needed to act quickly, so as to make the Great British Public aware that Madame

Tussauds were doing something incredible and new at Alton Towers. To do this, we agreed with the Planners that renovation and upgrading of existing attractions and facilities was the answer in the short term, but this would have to be quickly followed-up with a radically new and big attraction. So we landscaped the area around the existing Rapids ride, created pathways through it so that observers could enjoy watching its riders getting thoroughly soaked, themed it on an African theme ("Katanga Canyon") and added a Runaway Train powered coaster ride, which was routed around the Rapids water circuit.

Just over a little wooded hillock from the Rapids site was an abandoned works yard which had been a dumping ground for old machinery, containers and other redundant objects. It was neatly screened from view by trees on three sides. This site seemed ideal for the construction of a large dark ride building, which could be hidden by trees on three sides, and the ride's façade on the fourth side. Research showed that our visitors rather liked spooky things, and a Haunted House seemed to fit the bill.

Much has been written about Alton Towers' Haunted House attraction (and, indeed, a whole book has been published about it), but I'll briefly give you an insight into it.

Many theme parks around the world had developed spooky haunted dark rides. Most of these used what the industry termed "Endless" transit systems, which consisted of a continuous train of coupled cars which slowly progressed non-stop around a winding circuit. The advantage of this was that as they didn't stop in the station, the rate at which the vehicles entered and moved around the ride was enormous, and hence the throughput capacity of the attraction was very high (typically 2,000 riders per hour or more) which kept queues to a minimum. But I always felt that these rides lacked a sense of exploration and surprise. The riders were voyeurs not participants, and it was obvious to them that there was an endless procession of people in front and behind simply looking at the same thing as them. No events, surprises or shocks could manifest themselves on the journey.

Compare this to the dear little Ghost Train on Clacton Pier where you really felt ALONE! You were trundling around in pitch darkness, and suddenly things happened to YOU! Thrills, surprises, shocks at every twist and turn along the winding track. If only there were some way of combining this feeling of being a very small intimate group exploring a Haunted House, with the advantages of mass non-stop loading of an endless transit system. So I came up with the idea of individual 6-seater cars which progressed slowly non-stop through the station bumper-to-bumper, but as they entered the ride proper they would peel off from the cars behind, speed up considerably, and whizz through the ride and encounter the horrors within.

It was dead easy to come up with the idea, but another thing entirely to bring this to reality. We commissioned a German ride manufacturer who had experience in dark ride transit systems to design and build it, and the task proved very complicated indeed. Each of the 34 cars had its own on-board computer (accessed through a little hatch in the back of the car), and these computers communicated with the main master computer in the control room, monitoring the position and speed of every car around the circuit. If one car slowed down for any reason, the following car would sense this and position itself accordingly. It was a very sophisticated piece of technology.

But the transit system was only the means by which we moved our audience around the show. The most important thing was the show itself. Mike Jolly, head of marketing for the Tussauds Group, had appointed a new marketing manager for Alton Towers to mastermind the promotion of the newly-launched park. His name was Nick Varney, and he'd come from being brand manager at Rowntree Mackintosh. He didn't know anything about theme parks, but, boy, was he a quick learner! We worked well together as a team, and both Nick and I agreed that our Haunted House was going to be essentially a fun, family attraction. Although it would be "spooky", it would not have any elements of gore or horror. The acid test Nick wanted to apply was that no children should come out crying, and nobody would have nightmares as a result of visiting the Haunted House. So throughout the whole attraction humour would be the watchword.

So there was only one person in the lineup to build it ... Sparky!

Keith Sparkes came across from Colchester and I went through the layout plan and storyboard with him. He was amazed at the size and scale of the project (it was to be the biggest contract Sparkes Creative Services had ever tackled, and one of the largest dark rides of its kind in the world). We devised some very neat illusions that the riders would experience in the vestibule of the ride, including the ghost of a small child walking around inside a miniature doll's house, and a talking face (actually Sparky's own) in the flames of the fire, reciting a suitably doom-laden poem. The whole of this walkthrough pre-show was tilted in exactly the same way as Battersea Funfair's Crazy Cottage, and Barry Island's Whacky Goldmine, so the visitors had a strange disorientating off-balance sensation even before they boarded the ride.

The ride itself was enormous, and took the visitors through hallways, attics, cellars, a ballroom and eventually a haunted graveyard. Throughout the tour the visitors encountered all manner of diabolical manifestations and special effects. The Grand Official Opening was to take place on 31st March 1992, and TV celebrities Philip Schofield and Michaela Strachan were booked to officiate and perform for the TV cameras and press reporters who were going to be in attendance. But the day before the grand opening, one of the cars developed a fault. It's on-board computer kept cutting out, and needed re-setting wherever it had stopped in the ride by pressing a small button on its control panel reached through the hatch in the back of the car. The next morning, we all arrived at the Haunted House early to get it ready, and spray fresh cobwebs around, but as we started up the ride, another of the cars developed the same fault. Then another, and another. Each time a cutout went, the whole ride stopped and someone had to walk around the circuit to the find offending car and press its reset button to get it going again. The minutes were ticking by to the 11:00 opening ceremony. The TV cameras and reporters were in place, and Philip Schofield and Michaela Strachan had arrived at the administration office reception.

"What's the problem?" I said to Helmut, the German engineer. "Der Schaltkreis Sicherheitsabschaltung ist kaputt!" was his reply.

Oh joy! That's all I needed. All 34 Schaltkreis Sicherheitsabschaltungs (whatever they were!) were bust, and in 45 minutes we were to be on live national television. Then I had an idea. I radioed through to the office, "Get me 34 members of staff, anybody will do, send them over to the costume department, dress them up as undertakers, and whizz them over to the Haunted House. Quick!"

Philip Schofield and Michaela Strachan arrived at the front entrance to the Haunted House in a blaze of publicity and huge cheering crowds, and at the same time 34 "undertakers" arrived at the staff entrance around the back. I seated one in each car with the instructions to sit in a sinister pose in the rear seat with their hand nonchalantly dangling over the back of the car so that their finger could be in permanent contact with the reset button on the car's hidden control panel. "If the car stops," they were told, "PUSH THE BUTTON!"

We restarted the ride, the undertakers did what they were told and they kept the ride running. The tape was formally cut by the celebrities at the front door, everyone applauded, and thousands of people … visitors, journalists, VIP guests, and TV crews … poured in through the entrance, and rode through the ride accompanied by sinister characters in the back seat of each car. "What a brilliant idea to have those actors going around the ride with you," said one journalist. "It created a very spooky and surreal atmosphere. Pure genius!"

If only they'd known!

(By the way, 34 improved Schaltkreis Sicherheitsabschaltungs arrived the next day, and were duly fitted. The ride has run perfectly ever since!)

After the Haunted House had opened, we needed to work fast. In two years' time a big, new attraction had to debut to ensure that Alton Towers was put on the world theme park map. Something unique, something enormous, thrilling, amazing. … No pressure, then!

Because we had to keep everything we developed at Alton Towers below the height of the existing trees on the site, so as not to spoil views from the surrounding countryside, it was necessary to think outside the box. The obvious thing would have been to build an enormous high rollercoaster of world-beating dimensions, and we had the budget to do this. But the special nature of our site quite rightly prohibited this. And, in any case, we didn't want to do the obvious (we'd leave that to others!).

It was suggested by Andy Nichols that if we couldn't go up in the air, perhaps we could go down into the ground! We could dig an enormous hole on the site, and have the ride whizzing around down in the hole. "But do you realise how big this hole would have to be?" I asked Andy. "Gigantic?" was his reply.

But why not? Nobody had done it before. Provided we chose a location on the park where there were no existing trees, it wouldn't disturb the landscape. The geological consultants we had employed told us the ground was solid rock virtually throughout the site, so although it would be a massive job to excavate, the rock walls would be self-supporting. And the rock we excavated could be sold, or used to enhance the existing landscape elsewhere around the park.

But we still needed something different as the ride mechanism. I turned to Arrow Dynamics in America (who'd built the Vampire for us at Chessington) and they had just invented a "Pipeline" coaster. Whereas up to now rollercoasters had either rolled along <u>above</u> the track, or were suspended <u>beneath</u> it, in this novel concept, the cars would travel <u>between</u> the rails, as if you were rolling along a pipe.

The photographs that Arrow sent me of the prototype vehicles were bullet-shaped, reminiscent of some sort of high-tech missiles. They looked quite sinister in appearance, and the idea started to form in my mind of developing the whole themed ride area as a sinister secret military base where something rather unpleasant was being developed of which the rest of the world was to be kept oblivious. So I gave the attraction the codename "The Secret Weapon" and my first layout drawing was given the number "SW1".

I went out to Utah to ride the prototype in their works, and it was immediately apparent that this wasn't the ride for us. It was slow, cumbersome and boring. Back to the drawing board.

Then I heard through a good friend of mine, Stuart Cosgrove, (who is one of the most knowledgeable rollercoaster enthusiasts in the world), that a rather enigmatic Swiss company were secretly developing a completely new type of rollercoaster.

In any industry you have your regular manufacturers who produce products for the mass market, then you have one or two elite manufacturers who produce the top-of-the-range products, affordable only to those who value quality above price. Take the car industry: there are the main brand names (Ford, GM, Volkswagen etc.), but then at the very top are just a few elite brands (Lamborghini, Ferrari etc.) which most car lovers dream of owning. The same is true of the theme park industry. At the very top is an engineering company in Switzerland called Bolliger & Mabillard (known to everyone as B&M). They deliberately kept a very low profile, and never advertised their products. The big names in the theme park world knew who they were, and kept them very much under wraps. B&M produced the very best engineered rollercoasters in the world. (... Typical of the Swiss!).

I contacted them, and spoke to their principal director, Walter Bolliger. At first he was very wary of admitting that they were onto something new. But he had heard of Madame Tussauds (who hasn't!) and of Alton Towers, so after a lot of persuasion he agreed that Nick Varney and I could ride the prototype. When we saw it, we couldn't believe our eyes! This ride was doing the impossible! Up to now, regular coasters that rolled on top of the track could go upside down through loops and corkscrews. But here was a *suspended* coaster, inverted beneath the track, that was doing the same. What's more, there was nothing beneath the riders' feet! No floor to the car, just a suspended seat.

The ride was incredible. We rode it and rode it. Over and over again. This was the ride we just had to have!

We had earmarked an area near the old Thunderlooper at Alton Towers as suitable for our hole. The Thunderlooper was not the most beautiful of things (it had all the visual charm of a mini oil refinery), was dreadfully unreliable, and only had a temporary planning consent which was due to expire anyway. The potential site was bounded by tall mature trees at its perimeter, and our arboriculturalist surveyed these trees to plot the exact extent of their root-plates up to which we could excavate without interfering with them. After all, they did provide visual screening above ground level to enable the elevated track and structure to be concealed from off-site. Andy measured the trees and identified the tallest, next to which we should locate the highest point of the ride at the top of the rollercoaster's lift hill.

Badly designed rollercoasters tend to deliver their thrills in the completely opposite order to that which the basic laws of showmanship demand. A thrilling movie always saves the best and most exciting parts to the end ... the grand finale. But rollercoasters have their big thrills at the very beginning (after leaving the highest point of the lift hill) and the rest of the ride gets gradually tamer and tamer towards the end. I was determined that I would find a way to make sure the big thrills carried on right to the very end of the track. I did this by locating the station at a level halfway down the hole, so that I could still achieve some big dips and inversions down to the base of the excavation just before the train re-entered the station at the end of the ride. (This is something I have tried to achieve on all my subsequent coaster designs).

I obtained the track layout data from B&M which indicated the geometry of the various different track elements, and from this information I produced a track layout plan and profile to suit the site. I labeled this drawing "SW2" (and, incidentally, all new rollercoaster projects at Alton Towers have subsequently been given the "SW" prefix, right up to the present day). With some modifications from them, they then produced a three-dimensional "clearance envelope" which illustrated the exact extent their track and structure would require, and the excavation was designed. Peter Barber produced the necessary foundation designs, and digging started.

Nick and I had taken photos of the B&M prototype track, and it had a strange serpentine appearance. We wanted to weave a theme and story around the new attraction, and we had to be highly creative in this task. Indeed, Nick wanted to take this even further and create a 'brand' around the ride, which would include merchandise and other commercial spin-offs. We ditched the "Secret Weapon" idea, and came up with the concept that whilst excavating the site for something else we had supposedly disturbed a hideous monster that had been buried underground for millions of years. Its tentacles were writhing around in a snakelike manner (i.e. the rollercoasters' undulating track) and in order to control it, we had pinned it down with a steel structure (i.e. the supporting structure for the rollercoaster track). We got John Knowles at Madame Tussauds Studios to come up with some visuals to illustrate this, and everyone agreed this was a splendid theme. But we needed a name for this monster.

For days we pondered what it should be called. Various people on the project team put forward ideas, but we were getting nowhere. The deadline for starting the publicity campaign was nearing. Late one afternoon, I was walking past Nick Varney's office, and he grabbed me and pulled me inside. "The two of us are not leaving this office tonight until we've thought of a name," he said as he slammed the door shut behind us.

We sat at his desk, and looked blankly at each other for what seemed like hours. We thought about Greek mythological names, prehistoric monster names, ancient Egyptian pharaoh's names. Nothing was working. Then, on a book shelf behind him I saw the answer to our problem. It was not a dictionary, or reference book, or encyclopedia. It was a bottle of Southern Comfort. That should lubricate our creative juices.

By 8 o'clock the bottle was half empty, and the ideas were flowing. Our speech was becoming ever so slightly slurred. By 9 o'clock the bottle was empty, and Nick said "I don't care a f@©k what we call it, but it has to end in 'is'.

"Like Osiris?" I said.

"Yes, that sort of thing," he replied.

Now, normally people like to take the credit for successful things themselves. But what followed I distinctly remember came out of Nick's mouth, whereas he is convinced the name came out of mine. We give each other the credit for suddenly blurting out the name:

NEMESIS !

And the rest is history.

After the track installation was complete and the first train put on it, we prepared ourselves for the initial test run. Claude Mabillard (the "M" of "B&M") was leading the commissioning team of Swiss engineers. It was very apparent to everyone in the vicinity that something was about to happen. The word soon got around Alton Towers, and staff members from other departments started popping up all around the site to gape and watch the action. Claude and I naturally looked very anxious. Was it going to get round the track? Sandbags had been put in the train, and the lift motor was started. The brakes were released, and Nemesis climbed the lift hill. With a wonderful roar the massive train raced round the track at an amazing speed. It flew over the first inversion, around the bend under the monorail track, upside down over the station roof, through the vertical loop, deep down to the bottom of the excavation, up through the barrel roll, and into the station brakes.

Everyone cheered. It had made it!

But, of course, we knew it would, because we'd secretly run it at 2 o'clock the night before !

The following day after a few dozen more test runs, Claude sidled up to me and quietly whispered in perfect colloquial English "Care for a ride?"

"Try and stop me!" was my reply.

So we took the sandbags out of two of the front seats, and climbed aboard. Claude Mabillard and I were the very first people to ride Nemesis, and in the subsequent years we have been followed by over 22 million others.

On the day of the official opening, Nemesis behaved itself perfectly. Walter Bolliger (the "B" of "B&M") came over as an official guest, and one of ITV's TV 'Gladiators' performed the opening ceremony (and was violently sick afterwards, having consumed vast quantities of protein muscle-building drinks before embarking on the ride). I had to do the usual stuff for the TV cameras and the newspaper journalists, being portrayed as some kind of eccentric sadist who got his thrills out of scaring the living daylights out of people (which, in fact, is definitely not the case, but I go along with it, as that is what the publicity people seem to like).

But after the hullabaloo died down later in the afternoon, Walter and I were sat down together on a seat just underneath Nemesis's lift hill.

"You realise we've got a real problem here" I said to him.

He looked worried. "What do you mean?" he said.

"How the hell do we top this?" I replied.

At the top of Nemesis lift hill before the first ever run

Chapter 14

INTO OBLIVION

For the two years while we were building the Haunted House and the early stages of Nemesis, a film crew had been following me all around making a documentary about me and my work entitled "Themes, Dreams and Scream Machines". This went out on the national ITV network all over the country.

As a result, all sorts of people from my past contacted me. It was wonderful to re-new old acquaintances.

One day I took a phone call. The lady's voice on the phone said "Hello John. It's Dot from the windmill here."

Dot from the windmill? I didn't know any flour millers whose wives were called Dot. The name sounded like a character from Postman Pat, or Bob the Builder. Then the penny dropped. It was Dot Edwards, the box office manageress of the Windmill Theatre in Great Yarmouth.

"We all saw you on the telly the other night. Nobby, me, Bob Rayner. Even Mr. Jay saw you!"

We chatted away, and thought a Windmill reunion was called for. My wife Jenny and I were due to attend a conference in Norwich later that summer, so it was agreed we would get in touch nearer the time and organise something. So one day in July, a group of old Windmill Theatre staff got together for the first time in 26 years in the bar of the Star Hotel on Hall Quay in Great Yarmouth. And none of us had changed a bit! During the course of the reminiscences, Bob Rayner said "Mr. Jay has followed your career with interest, you know."

I was amazed. I had assumed that he had long-forgotten the gawky 18-year-old lad who had flyposted his way around Great Yarmouth for him. "We've told him we're meeting you today, and I know he'd love to see you. He's very frail now."

A quick phone call was made, and it was arranged that Jenny and I would call at noon the following day on Mr. and Mrs. Jay at the home they still lived in on Marine Parade in Great Yarmouth. It was with some trepidation that I rang the doorbell, not knowing what to expect. The elderly gentleman that answered the door was immediately recognizable. He was in his late 80's and did indeed look frail, as did his wife Freda, but they were most welcoming and genuinely seemed to appreciate our visit. They had even got in a bottle of wine for the occasion, which they cracked open specially for us. We had a wonderful hour together, and Mr. Jay obviously really had followed my career, since he seemed to know all about what I'd been up to for the previous two decades.

His eyes became heavy, and it was obvious that he was getting tired. Although we could have carried on reminiscing and talking for hours, I felt it was not fair on him for us to stay any longer. So we got up to leave.

"Well, Mr. Jay" I said, "It's been wonderful to see you again"

What he said in reply has stayed at the front of my memory ever since.

"Please don't call me Mr. Jay. Call me Jack."

Even as I type this now, tears fill my eyes. Here was one of the most respected entertainment entrepreneurs of his day, and he was raising me up to the status of one of his peers. This was the greatest accolade anyone could give me, and the zenith of my career.

....

No sooner had Nemesis opened than Ray Barratt asked me to go over to Spain, and investigate a project in which Tussauds were considering investing. The owners of Barcelona's mountain-top amusement park, Tibidabo, had got funding from the large Spanish bank La Caixa to develop a theme park on a site about 60 miles southwest of the city, near the coastal resort of Salou. It was to be called "Tibi Gardens".

They had acquired as a financial partner a well-known American brewery who operated theme parks in the States. As it turned out, there were major cultural differences of opinion between the Catalan management and their American partners. To reconcile these differences it was felt that a third party was required to "bridge the cultural gap" – one who knew something about theme park operation but was also European in culture. Tussauds were considered ideal for this role.

I was sent, together with Peter Selinger from Tussauds head office, as the initial scouts. Peter was to investigate the commercial prospects of the project, and I was to examine and report back on the overall park layout, its rides, and shows.

What we found was an enormous dustbowl of a site, on which mountains had been moved and vast pits dug. The model which was displayed to us was a thing of beauty, and obviously had got bankers, financiers and everyone who held judgement over the project completely dewy-eyed. But the rides themselves looked rather irrational in their design. The layouts seemed over-complicated, but at the same time rather dull. They looked as if they had been designed by architects, not entertainers. Some contracts had already been signed, and it was too late to do anything about them. These included a huge runaway mine train, a logflume, and a spillwater splash ride. I phoned back to Ray to tell them that if we were to consider investing in the project, the developers were to be told to immediately halt any further ride contract negotiations.

We returned to London with cases full of plans and documents. The main ride contract which concerned me most was the star-turn attraction of the whole park, a gigantic rollercoaster. It was ill-conceived, and not dissimilar to a ride the American partner had built in one of its own parks nearly 20 years earlier. I felt sure we could do better than that, but time was not on our side. The park was due to open the following year.

We had been delighted with all the dealings we had had at Alton Towers with B&M on the Nemesis project, both in terms of the quality of the engineered product, and their efficient and pleasant management style. So I contacted Walter Bolliger and asked if he'd be interested in designing a big new rollercoaster for this Spanish park. He said yes, and we worked together to produce a layout and profile for the ride which would eventually be built and called Dragon Khan. I spent much time in Spain over the next 12 months, and Tussauds sent a large management team out there to permanently manage the project. The Catalan people were a pleasure to work with, and gave me a new perspective on aspects of my work which would influence my thinking on future projects. Eventually the park opened, and its name was changed to PortAventura.

Thinking of the future, I needed to come up with ideas for new rides for both the second phase of Port Aventura and also Alton Towers. I was convinced a wooden rollercoaster would provide just what both parks needed. "Woodies" were spectacular, fun, thrilling and very different from anything either of the parks already had. I talked this over with Ray Barratt and he agreed that I should do some investigation into the matter. It was at this very time that William McNamara from Oakwood got in touch with me and asked my advice on what their next big attraction should be. I sensed this was an opportunity for me to help develop a wood coaster for him which could lead to further developments at our own parks. A woodie would be ideal for Oakwood. It fitted in to the woodland landscape perfectly, it was an exciting yet family-friendly ride, and much of the labour and materials to construct it could be sourced locally in Britain.

William and I contacted wooden coaster manufacturers in the U.S.A., and we made a tour of various parks around the eastern states, including Kennywood, Cedar Point and Kings Island to ride their wooden coasters. Custom Coasters of Cincinnati were selected as the chosen manufacturer, and I worked with them to design and build what would become Megafobia, the signature coaster at Oakwood.

So in the second phase of its development I realised my dream to build a big racing wooden rollercoaster at PortAventura. As with all my rides, I wanted as much engagement as possible from the riders and spectators, which is why I proposed a twin-track racer (where two trains run side-by-side on parallel tracks and compete in a race to the finish). This was not unique in the world, and so I added an extra twist. Halfway round the circuit the trains entered a tunnel. On emerging from the tunnel, the two tracks appeared to be the same as before, but suddenly the other train came straight towards you in the opposite direction as if you were on a collision course! It whizzed past, you entered a second tunnel, and the tracks came together again for the finish of the race.

We called the ride The Stampeda. It was very thrilling, but not suitable for small children. So I added a third kiddy-track (called The Tomahawk) with its own little train, which joined the race at the very end (and the little kiddies often won the race!).

Tussauds Studios in London had enjoyed working on the artistic design and theming of Nemesis, and were beginning to realise that perhaps theme park work wasn't beneath them after all! From this point on, they took an increasingly influential role in the design of the attractions for Chessington World of Adventures, Alton Towers and PortAventura. Eventually they assigned dedicated art directors to these parks, firstly Paul Lanham, and latterly Candy Holland. This freed up much more of my time as things were starting to expand.

Just around the M25 from Chessington World of Adventures was the "opposition" in the form of Thorpe Park. They were a thorn in our side, as they shared the same family market as our park, and many of their attractions duplicated ours. By this time, Mike Jolly had become Chief Executive of the Tussauds Group, and Jill Britten had taken over his role of Group Director of Marketing. Jill and I decided we would sneak into Thorpe Park incognito as paying visitors, and have a good look around to see if the park might be worth buying.

It was a rainy day, so, suitably disguised in anoraks with hoods pulled over our heads, we toured Thorpe Park, blending in with the other visitors. We went on most of the rides, but apparently a ride operator on their indoor rollercoaster (called "X No Way Out") spotted me amongst the crowds on a CCTV security camera in the ride. He was a rollercoaster enthusiast called Dave McCubbin, and he'd seen me on television. In no time at all the word was all round Thorpe Park that Tussauds were there. We'd been rumbled!

I subsequently produced a report on the existing rides at the park, and how we might further expand the attraction so as to complement rather than compete with Chessington. This was accepted by the Tussauds Board, and, as a consequence, we did indeed buy Thorpe Park. From that moment on, Chessington World of Adventures and Thorpe Park were able to divide the market sensibly between themselves, and not be in opposition to one another.

One day a television scriptwriter called Rob Heyland contacted me. He had written a TV drama series about an architect who had an affair with his female assistant whilst working on a project abroad, two-timing his wife as a consequence. The BBC had accepted this for production and transmission, but felt that the profession of architect didn't give sufficient scope for insightful events and unusual locations. He therefore decided that he would re-write the whole story and change the main character from an architect to a theme park designer. He had seen me being interviewed on television, and asked me if I could help him and act as script advisor. I said we should meet to talk about this.

He visited my home, we went through his existing script, and he asked me lots of probing question about the theme park industry and my work. Then he posed a question that completely caught me off-guard: "May I base the lead character on YOU?"

"But I'm a perfectly happily married man. I'm not having an affair with my assistant and I have no intention of two-timing my wife!" I exclaimed. He said the character would be based purely on my professional life, not on my personal one. I called Jenny into the room and asked her for her opinion. We all agreed that provided it was made absolutely clear, in any publicity material that mentioned me, that it was only as a theme park designer that I was portrayed, and that any similarity stopped there!

For the next three months, draft scripts went back and forth between us as I made suggestions and corrections. I met with the director, Paul Seed, and discussed suitable theme park locations. Eventually it was arranged that the main location would be PortAventura in Spain, and that the construction project in the story which my character was working on would be the Dragon Khan rollercoaster, the coaster I had actually constructed a few years earlier in real life. The production was cast, and Miles Anderson got the role of Sam Dawson (my character), Sinead Cusack his wife and Holly Aird his mistress.

The director asked Miles Anderson to meet up with me to get under the skin of the character he was to play. I spent the day with him at Alton Towers, showing him the rides and explaining how I set about designing them. But his approach to the part went deeper than that, and I felt he was watching my every move, my body language, how I ate my lunch, what I was wearing, how I talked to people. It was very strange and disconcerting.

My wife, Jenny, had been a TV vision mixer before we married, and coincidentally knew the director, Paul Seed. It was agreed that Jenny and I would go out to Spain with the production unit during the filming, with me acting as technical advisor, and both of us playing bit-parts as necessary.

Filming commenced, first in the U.K. then we all flew out to Spain and had a really fun week at PortAventura. It was bizarre when

Miles Anderson kept turning to me during different shots and asking how I'd speak, react or behave under similar circumstances. The production went out on BBC television as a four-part mini-series entitled 'Have Your Cake And Eat It' over two consecutive weekends, and got good viewing figures. It also went on to win a Royal Television Society award.

Soon it was time for Alton Towers to have another big ride. But, as always, it had to be very different, not just from anything existing on the park, but also a world's first. I was convinced that a wooden coaster would be a sensational hit but the Tussauds board were very skeptical. Their market research indicated that the public thought wooden coasters were old-fashioned and unsafe. Furthermore, it would be difficult to make such a coaster a world's first. I was certain that a well-designed wooden coaster would very quickly become a popular attraction at the park, and word-of-mouth would spread its good reputation rapidly. That, unfortunately, wasn't good enough, and I was told in no uncertain terms to look for something else.

Walter Bolliger had spoken to me in the past about an idea for a vertical drop coaster. The problem we had was the same one we had for Nemesis – lack of height. But that was not the first hurdle we needed to overcome.

In order to help you understand the unique problem when designing a vertical drop rollercoaster, I need you to do a little experiment.

Find yourself a string of beads (preferably not a set of valuable pearls) and lay them on a polished table top. Now slowly pull one end of the string over the edge of the table and down towards the floor. As you pull more of the beads over the edge, their own weight will take over and the string will accelerate. By the time the last bead is passing over the edge of the table top, it will be moving forward with enormous speed, and instead of simply changing to a downward direction it will be projected forward. Now imagine that the string of beads is a long rollercoaster train. After the first car has gone over the precipice the increasing weight of the train will accelerate it, so that the passengers in the last carriage will be hurled forwards as they start the descent. That is the issue. And the longer the train, the greater the problem.

So we decided that if we were to achieve a vertical drop rollercoaster with a high capacity train, that train should be very short in length. This dictated that if it couldn't be long, it would have to be wide to get the same number of seats in. So the vehicles on the new ride were designed to be eight seats wide, by two rows deep. Nobody had ever designed a rollercoaster with such an unusual train design before.

The next problem was height, and again, if we couldn't go up, we'd have to go down: underground this time, (Nemesis had descended below ground level into a quarried excavation, but hadn't actually gone underground). It was an audacious concept, but worth a try. The riders would drop vertically downwards into a gaping hole in the ground, and disappear into oblivion. This time Southern Comfort wasn't needed to help us come up with the name: Oblivion.

The concept of the ride was very straightforward and could easily be marketed by Alton's new marketing director Glenn Earlam (by now Nick Varney had moved on to start a visitor attraction empire of his own). Glenn needed to put over the simple idea that you got on a vehicle, were lifted up very high, and then dropped vertically downwards straight into a gaping hole in the ground. However I felt we needed to add an extra twist. There was no doubt that looking down from the top of the drop would be a very daunting sight, so why not make the most of this, and pause the vehicle on the brink for just a couple of seconds to build up the tension. A simple enough idea, but an enormously costly one to achieve.

To hold the massively heavy vehicle and its passengers over the brink of the drop involved adding an extra chain conveyor to this section of the track, with reverse-acting chain engagement dogs to every car (please forgive these unwieldy technical terms, but some readers might be impressed by them). All this added an extra £350,000 to the cost of the ride hardware, but it was money well-spent (as millions of subsequent riders of Oblivion will testify). In addition, we decided that during this pause, a recorded announcement would be played through loudspeakers adjacent to the vehicle which said in an ominous voice: "DON'T ... LOOK ... DOWN !". As yet another diabolical feature, I decided that we'd fill the underground tunnel itself with cold, wet fog which would overflow up through the tunnel mouth to make it look all the more terrifying.

One thing which was concerning me when we were building the ride and digging the enormous tunnel into which it would drop was the issue of air pressure shockwaves. Have you noticed that when you are in a train that suddenly enters a tunnel, your ears pop as the shockwave of the fast-moving train rams into the static air in the tunnel? Well, I was concerned that this might be the case on Oblivion, but to a greater degree. We got experts to do calculations and they all said it wouldn't be an issue, but I decided that if anyone was going to have their eardrums burst on the very first ride around the track, it should be me. I mentioned this to Martin Booth who was the head of engineering at Alton Towers, and he said he too wanted to be a guinea-pig.

Once again, Claude Mabillard was B&M's commissioning engineer on the project, and after the usual sandbag tests he decided that Oblivion was ready to ride it's first human passengers. As with Nemesis, this had to be done in a somewhat covert way. When a ride is being tested over and over again with sandbags it is rather an uninteresting sight and nobody takes much notice. But as soon as the word gets around that someone's going to ride it, everybody stops what they're doing to watch. And that means not just everyone working on the construction site, not just everyone working at Alton Towers, but also most of Uttoxeter, Cheadle, Ashbourne, and half of Staffordshire! So when Claude whispered to me "Let's give it ride!" I said "Hold on. I promised Martin Booth the first run with us."

By this time Claude had stopped the ride and was about to remove some sandbags. Martin was not on the site but was somewhere on the other side of the huge theme park, so I radioed him with a suitably obtuse coded message that only he would understand: "Get over to Oblivion straight away for something to your advantage!"

The minutes ticked by, Claude made it look as if he'd stopped the ride running so he could make some subtle adjustment, and then Martin arrived puffing and panting having run all the way from the logflume. We pulled out three sets of sandbags and climbed into three of the front seats, and we were off! For the first time in my life on a rollercoaster I was genuinely scared. Nobody had ever dropped vertically into a small hole in the ground like this before. We reached the top. "DON'T ... LOOK ...DOWN !" said the voice as we paused at the top. But we did look down. Of course we did! Everyone does!

And then:

" Wooooaaaahhhh!"

We dropped down and down, and entered the cold dark tunnel into Oblivion. The huge "G" forces which we experienced as the vehicle pulled through the bend deep underground before emerging back into the daylight moments later were incredible to experience. The vehicle arrived back in the station exactly as predicted, and we discovered that fortunately our eardrums hadn't burst, and the pressure shockwave wasn't an issue after all.

The year was 1998.

Shortly after Oblivion opened, Mike Jolly, Tussauds Group Chief Executive, asked if I could go to meet him at the Group's head offices above Maple's furniture store in Tottenham Court Road in London. I sensed something important was afoot. By this time I was a non-executive director of four of the companies within the Tussauds Group. He explained that Pearsons had decided that they wanted to consolidate their portfolio of subsidiary companies, and concentrate on their core business of publishing and media. This meant selling-off all the odd-ball companies like Tussauds. And when this happened all the non-executive directors would have to resign. He explained that this shouldn't really affect me, as I could continue my relationship with the company as a freelance consultant. I was perfectly happy with the situation.

The Group was now actively developing new rides at Alton Towers, Thorpe Park and Chessington World of Adventures, and my time was very gainfully employed. Although the next big new ride at Alton Towers wasn't scheduled to open till 2002, we had no time to lose. Again, I was told it had to be a "world's first". Various different ride manufacturers around the world had tried to invent new types of rollercoaster with varying degrees of success, but most had been unappealing, uncomfortable or unreliable. We had had exceptionally good experiences with B&M developing both Nemesis and Oblivion (and B&M had done very nicely out of selling subsequent models of these rides to other parks in America and the Far East), and it was decided that if we were to try and pioneer a third completely novel ride attraction for Alton Towers, we would develop it with them.

So I went to their offices in Monthey, at the eastern end of Lake Geneva, in Switzerland, for a brainstorming session.

The magnificent Rhône valley empties its powerful river into lake Geneva in a rather lazy way. One minute it is a rapid torrent, foaming and white, the next minute it's lost all its energy and it slumps into the lake without a fuss. And the industrial town of Monthey is located just before it does this. Anywhere else on earth, chimneys of chemical works and bulky factories would look ugly, but here in Monthey

they are dwarfed beneath the majestic backdrop of the Alps, and the town is a rather agreeable place. And on its outskirts are the anonymous and somewhat under-stated head offices of Bolliger & Mabillard.

I sat down around the table with the principles of the company, Walter and Claude, and their chief designers. It wasn't long before we all agreed that our goal was fairly obvious. In the past people had ridden rollercoasters above the track and below the track in a seated position. If only there were some way to ride a rollercoaster suspended beneath the track laying face down in a FLYING position! Like Superman! We hadn't a clue how we were going to do it, but it had to be possible somehow. It would need some sort of clever harness arrangement, that would fit everybody from a smallish child to an obese adult. It had to be comfortable, it had to be quick (or virtually instant) to get into, and, most importantly, it had to be completely safe. The task was an onerous one.

We all scribbled ideas and sketches on pieces of paper which were passed around and thoroughly discussed, and eventually a way forward was agreed. But not before something fundamental was established. Secrecy. The theme park industry was huge, and competition between both parks and amongst ride manufacturers was fierce. It was vital that no other park should find out what Alton Towers were proposing to debut in 2002, and no other ride manufacturer should get wind of what B&M were developing for them. Only those people in the room at that moment in time would be party to the secret at B&M's end, and just a small handful of people at the Alton / Tussauds end.

Over the next few months, sketches of the proposed car and harness were faxed back and forth between myself, Martin Booth, and B&M. And then the time came for Martin and me to make another visit to Switzerland to try out the prototype. The security under which this technology was being developed was amazing. A special workshop had been set up deep inside their nearby factory complex, 24-hour security guards kept away intruders, and only the two engineers working in this special development facility were privy to what was going on within. The car essentially looked like a Nemesis suspended seat arrangement, and I got in. But that's where the similarity ended. Various adjustable metal rods and soft foam pads had been added to create a special harness. Added to this, a flexible jacket moved downwards into place and pressed against my chest, and clamps swung round and held my ankles. Then, the two engineers released a locking mechanism, and manually tilted the whole assembly backwards, pivoting from above, so that I was now face down to the ground.

I was only three feet from the ground, and at first it was a most disconcerting sensation. But extraordinarily enough, I felt comfortable and secure. They tilted me back upright again, released my containment, and Martin got in to give it a try.

There was still a long way to go, but it looked very encouraging. It all had to operate automatically and be self adjusting. And it had to be completely fail-safe, with mechanical locking devices incorporating triple redundancy and electronic monitoring sensors. These trains would be by far the most technically sophisticated and expensive rollercoaster trains in the world. And it was vital that nobody should discover how we were doing this till the first guests rode the ride on opening day. Then the secret would be out.

Work started on the site at Alton Towers to construct the foundations of the new ride, and the development team was formed to consider how the attraction was to be branded and marketed. Whereas both Nemesis and Oblivion were promoted as "villains" (in other words, some sort of adversarial foe you had to overcome) it was decided that the new ride would instead be the "hero". It enabled you to do something you always wanted to do: fly.

So we decided to give it an upbeat non-confrontational name …

AIR !

Testing the prototype "AIR" harness
at Bolliger & Mabillard's Swiss factory

Whilst the ride track and support structure were being assembled on site, the word got around the internet that Alton Towers were indeed building a "flying coaster" with B&M, and there was much speculation as to how the cars were going to load their passengers quickly, safely and comfortably, whilst putting the riders in this extraordinary flying position. This would obviously be revealed when the trains arrived onsite, so precautions were taken to ensure that they could not be seen until we were ready to make the first test run.

Chapter 15

AIR TODAY – GONE TOMORROW

With the "Air" project well-underway at Alton Towers, the news came through that Pearsons had, indeed, sold the Tussauds Group to a venture capital company. I was no longer a director, and, ironically twelve months later none of my old executive director colleagues would be either. I had naively assumed that a management buy-out meant that the management was in control. But, of course, in actual fact the financiers who hold the purse strings have the real power, and they decided that a completely new board of directors was required to fulfill their financial aspirations.

So virtually overnight all my old colleagues vanished from the scene. It was a very sad occasion to see people with whom I had worked for many years, and who loved and understood the business, cast to the wind. For the time being it was "business as usual" for me, as I was heavily involved in the completion of "Air" and also "Colossus" at Thorpe Park, and I continued to design wooden coasters for Alton Towers in the hope that one day the management would see some sense!

However, once these new rides opened, the entirely new senior board of management felt that the ride design team led by Candy Holland at Tussauds Studios in London were perfectly capable of designing any new rides themselves without outside help or interference from me. In fact, this was absolutely right. Candy was an incredibly competent attraction designer with a very dynamic and imaginative team of people behind her. From time-to-time they would ask me to produce a layout for a possible new coaster, but, for five years from 2002, I considered myself happily retired.

But in 2007 the news broke in the trade press that Merlin Entertainments Ltd. had bought the Tussauds Group from the venture capitalists. Merlin had grown from a small cluster of Sealife Centres and Dungeon attractions to become one of the world's largest attraction operators, and at its head was none other than Nick Varney. Shortly after the deal had been done Nick was assessing his new assets, and he asked someone "Where's John Wardley?". I guess people must have shrugged their shoulders, and muttered things like "I think he does a bit for Candy at the Studios from time to time"

So Nick phoned me up. "What's going on?" he asked. I explained that I'd retired, and he asked me if I'd like to return as a consultant to the company. I agreed, and found myself back with my old friends including Mark Fisher who was to run the theme park division for Merlin (and whom I'd worked with at Alton Towers when we first bought the park) and Glenn Earlam. Once again, our parks were owned by a company who realised that if you put as your main priority the entertainment of your guests, the money would be made.

In the years that followed I played only a very small part in the development of new rides within the Group, although the parks' marketeers found me a useful person to put in front of the press and TV cameras when they were launching a new attraction. The media like to home-in on one personality as the "creator" of something new, and I would have to play this role. I often felt very uncomfortable doing this, as in actual fact the people who should have been taking all the credit were Candy and her team back in London. But fortunately she understood the reality of the situation. Although I did produce the layouts and profiles for subsequent rides at Alton, Thorpe, Heide Park and Gardaland, the real creator of these rides was Candy Holland.

Nick Varney was, first and foremost, a marketing man, and his main criteria when judging any new ideas for theme park rides and attractions was for us all to consider two things:

1) What is the compelling proposition (i.e. what is the unique selling point, in just a few words)?

2) What is the "killer image" (i.e. what single image of the ride conveys that compelling proposition)?

Unless both these criteria could be satisfied, the concept would fall at the first hurdle.

This basic philosophy was applied to Alton's next major ride. We needed to do something with a rollercoaster that had never been done before. But it had to be relevant to the ride experience and entertaining for the riders. In the past, coaster trains had dropped down vertical slopes along the track, but never before had the actual track itself dropped. The Swiss manufacturer Intamin had developed the technology for their "Freefall" towers which allowed a massive free-falling load to be safely braked to a smooth halt using magnetic brakes. They suggested an entire section of coaster track, complete with a train on it, could be caused to fall in the same way. Not only that, but I suggested that perhaps the train could then accelerate backwards after its descent, and negotiate the remaining portion of the circuit in reverse. And all this could be done within a large building, in semi-darkness!

Again, the sensitivity of the Alton Towers site was a major consideration. The Corkscrew ride had been at the park since 1980 and it was felt that it was time for its retirement. It had nostalgia-value, but its popularity had declined since Nemesis, Oblivion and Air had opened. So it was agreed with the local planning authority that if a new ride was to be built at the park, it should occupy the site which the Corkscrew had vacated.

Unfortunately, the old Corkscrew was a very compact ride which occupied a relatively small space. And as the years went by, Alton Towers' rides were getting bigger, better, and more exciting. So it was going to be necessary for us to extend the footprint of the new ride outside the boundaries of the existing site and into the woodland to the south. The planners made it clear to us that any major construction should be contained on the old Corkscrew site, and that only "runaway" track with minimal structure would be permissible in the woodland. Furthermore, all track and structure had to be kept below the existing tree canopy and not be visible from outside the park boundaries.

This suggested two themes. Any large buildings which contained the station and drop track would need to be heavily disguised or decorated, and it was felt that a structure in the same architectural style as the original Pugin-designed Towers would be appropriate. But also if the ride were to whizz off through the woodland, and take the riders on a high-speed dash through the trees, some sort of forest theme should be integrated into this. Candy and the team at the Studios got to work and came up with the brilliant idea of the forest taking over the old derelict building, and causing it to collapse.

This was where I came in to configure the track. The ride would leave the station, proceed up a lift to tree-top height, and then go through the woodland at high speed, weaving through the trees, narrowly missing the branches. It would then re-enter the building at a high level, the track would drop down to basement level, and the train would then be propelled backwards in total darkness around a twisting and undulating underground tunnel. A reversing track would then accelerate the train in a forward direction and return to the station. Eventually a layout and profile was agreed, and Intamin started fabrication of the steelwork.

One stipulation we made was that before any track was delivered to the site, we had to test the completely novel drop section and approve the effect it delivered before any further work was undertaken. This was to be done at the steel fabrication factory in Budapest, and in due course we paid a visit to the factory to experience the drop for ourselves.

Our first view of the drop track
at the fabricators in Budapest

With great trepidation we climbed the scaffolding tower, and strapped ourselves into the seats which were fixed to the track at the top. Then a count-down took place, and we plummeted down to the ground. Having experienced this amazing sensation, we were in no doubt that this was going to be an incredible and thrilling ride, especially as the drop was going to be done in complete darkness amid a plethora of diabolical special effects which Candy had up her sleeve!

Not only was the ride going to be unique, so was its name.

TH13TEEN

After TH13TEEN opened, we had discussions with B&M about developing yet another new rollercoaster product with them. Traditionally, coasters had run above the track and below the track. Now we wanted to develop a coaster that ran either side of the track, so that the riders would have nothing above them, and nothing below them. The vehicle would therefore be very wide (as it overhung either side of the track), but also very low. In this way it could pass through narrow "slots" in the scenery, and rapidly tip on its side to pass through slim vertical openings as well as low horizontal apertures. The "Wing Coaster" concept was born.

Candy had asked me to work on the layouts for new Wing Coasters for Gardaland and Thorpe Park, and shortly after Thorpe's ride 'The Swarm' opened I was contacted by a TV production company who were making a series of programmes for Discovery Channel about people with weird and unusual jobs. They considered me to be a suitable subject!

Thorpe Park was looking for more exposure for their new ride so it was agreed that filming would take place there. I met the director, Tim Usborne (who had a very impressive portfolio of previous productions including BBC science documentaries) at the park and filming commenced. He wanted me to explain the science behind rollercoaster rides, including G-forces, centrifugal forces and so on. I had felt that in order to do this properly I would need someone to demonstrate various experiments whilst I talked through the science behind them. Tim had therefore arranged for a young lady, Emma Bassett, to come along and fulfill this role. I assumed she was an aspiring actress as she played her part extremely well throughout the day.

Towards the end of the day's filming, Tim lined up a shot of myself and Emma in closeup, with the Colossus rollercoaster (which I'd designed several years earlier) in the background. I thought this was rather odd, as all the other filming had been done on the new "Swarm" wing-coaster, but he was insistent that this particular ride must be in shot. Then whilst the camera was running he said to Emma, "Emma, could you tell John why his rollercoasters are so important to you."

What followed stunned me.

Emma said: "Several years ago I started to get headaches, and my doctor sent me to hospital to have a brain scan. They discovered a tumour in my brain the size of a satsuma. But they said something had happened to me during the previous week that had caused the fluid in the tumour to start to disperse and release the pressure in my brain. If this hadn't happened I'd have been dead by then. They asked me what event might have caused this. I told them I'd been to Thorpe Park and on the Colossus rollercoaster with my friends, and they said that had saved my life."

"What do you think of that, John?" the director asked as the cameras were rolling. For once I was speechless. Perhaps designing theme park rides isn't so fatuous and puerile after all.

Then it was time to start thinking about Alton Towers next big ride to open in 2013. I decided that this would be the last ride I would be involved in before my final (?) retirement. The previous year the park had conducted a survey amongst the general public of what the most popular rides at Alton Towers were, and, perversely, the three oldest rides came out top ... Nemesis, Oblivion and Air. It seemed wrong to me, since the latest and most up-to-date attractions should always be the most popular, even though the poll-toppers were "my" rides! So we all agreed, whatever the new ride for 2013 was going to be, it was going to be big, different, spectacular and thrilling.

Candy Holland and her team at Merlin's studios in London and I had numerous brain-storming sessions. What did Alton Towers not have in the way of rollercoasters, and did the new ride have to be a rollercoaster anyway? The answer to this last question was indisputable. Yes, rollercoasters really captured the public's imagination and were considered the signature attractions at the park. But what type of rollercoaster? The industry had developed stand-up coasters, but they weren't as thrilling to ride as people imagined. It was vital the new ride had to exceed the guests' expectations, so any attraction that might under deliver was out of the question. A wing coaster would be appropriate, but that would steal the thunder from Thorpe Park as we had developed one there the previous year. We all knew that a traditional wooden coaster would be an absolutely perfect attraction for the park, and would thrill young and old alike, but the public's pre-conceptions of them being old-fashioned kept coming back to haunt us. I was convinced that once the guests had ridden such a ride they would love it and be very enthusiastic. Alton Towers had just employed a talented new marketing director whom I was confident had the ability to market such an attraction. But unfortunately yet again the weight of opinion went against me.

So we then embarked on a crazy blue-sky approach, considering all sorts of novel off-the-wall ideas ... ball coasters that rolled along the track with the riders inside a ball ... trackless coasters guided by goodness-knows-what ...coasters with double-decker trains so that you could choose whether you rode on top of the track or underneath it ... trains that were made up of various combinations of different seating arrangements (stand-up, sit-down, backwards, floorless etc.) so you could choose how you rode it ... the ideas flowed, but nothing seemed to be working (and we didn't have any time to spare to undertake research and development for new technology). Then we looked at various sites around the park where a big coaster would fit, and where we were most likely to obtain Planning Consent from Staffordshire Moorlands Council. The precious weeks and months were ticking by. Over the years of developing new rides at Alton Towers, we knew that the build-program for a new rollercoaster was 18 months from breaking ground on site to having a reliable, safe, fully-commissioned rollercoaster ready for public operation.

In the end, as time was getting very tight, it was decided that the least-contentious planning site was the location previously occupied by the old Black Hole indoor coaster. But what was going to be it's U.S.P. (unique selling point)? People seemed to be fascinated by upside-down inversions in rollercoasters. We had created the world record-breaking coaster with the most inversions, Colossus at Thorpe Park, which had 10 inversions. Doubtless, someone somewhere was planning to beat that with an 11- or 12-inversion coaster. We certainly couldn't have 13, as that would create a confusing message with the previous ride, TH13TEEN. So we decided if we were going to have a record-breaker we would do it in style ... with 14 inversions!

But how were we going to squeeze that number of upside-down loops into the relatively small space of the old Black Hole site? And, from my knowledge of designing coasters, I knew that each inversion takes up a certain amount of lift energy from the train. 14 inversions would require a lift height of at least 50m., and there was no way the local planning authority would let us develop a structure of this height which would stick up above the trees, and be seen for miles around. But we could divide the ride into two separate sections, each with its own lift hill. And those two lifts could each be different in character – one inclined, and one vertical. And we could raise the station up and have a barrel-roll under the station in the dark as a prelude to the ride. The ideas were starting to shape up nicely.

Andy Nichols did some sightline calculations by sending up helium balloons to see whereabouts on the site the highest points of the structure would still be concealed by the existing trees. This was the technique we had used for all our previous coasters. The red balloons were sent up on strings, and Andy would tour the surrounding countryside with his camera, photographing the resulting views as the rest of us walked around the site, communicating with him on our mobile phones, raising and lowering the balloons and changing their positions until they could no longer be seen. This determined that the tops of the two lifts had to be at the eastern end of the site, and the station should be at the lowest part of the site to the west. Slowly, a rough layout and profile was coming together in my mind. I sent Candy Holland a preliminary computer simulation of this layout, and we shortlisted a number of manufacturers who were approached to come up with some proposals. One of these was selected, who amended my track layout and profile somewhat, and Candy and I then worked on this to maximise the thrill factor, ensuring that the 14 inversions were included, but in such a way that anybody looking at the drawings we were submitting for the planning application could not count the number of inversions and determine it was a record-breaker ... this was to be our secret!

Once the layout and profile of the ride had been finalised, Candy and her team set-to in conjunction with the marketing guys at Alton Towers to consider the name and theme of the ride. This was where I took a step back and prepared for my impending retirement.

The deadline for the 18-month build program had long past, and the construction team were now in uncharted territory trying to contract the program into a very tight schedule. The next twelve months saw massive hurdles and problems overcome on site, as one of the coldest and hardest winters on record hit Staffordshire. The theme of the ride was to be a sort of Orwellian nightmare scenario where a sinister organisation would take over the minds and bodies of the riders and combine optical illusions and mind-bending effects with the physical thrills of the ride. The attraction was to be called "The Smiler". All this was very clever, and in capable hands. I did not return to the project until a few months before the ride was due to open, and I was put forward as its "creator" for the purposes of press, TV and other PR activities. I played this rôle as best I could, aware that many other people had far more involvement in the ride than I, and were far more qualified to be nominated as its creator. Two months before the ride was scheduled to open I was locked in a cramped radio studio in London for a day and did 18 live radio interviews, one after the other, to promote the ride on various radio stations around the country. No matter how much I tried to correct them, the presenters still introduced me as the person who (apparently single-handedly!) designed, created, and built the world's most amazing new rollercoaster which was soon to open at Alton Towers. I could not help but visualise the hundreds of people who were out in the freezing cold pouring tons of concrete, battling with massive chunks of steel, or designing and constructing huge decorative pieces of scenery for the ride whilst I sat in the comfort of a radio studio taking all the credit.

The huge construction problems had meant that the ride was far behind schedule, and everything was very last-minute. I visited the site on several occasions, and was amazed at everyone's optimism on how the technical commissioning of the ride could be telescoped into a fraction of the time that had been allowed on other previous projects. The beginning of the 2013 season had commenced and the ride was nowhere near ready for opening. Eventually it was decided that ITV's breakfast show would have the weather presented from Alton Towers on 10th. May and I was asked to be there to be interviewed. Early that morning, the ride got its safety certificate for us to ride it, and Keith Workman, the Smiler's Project Manager, asked if I would like to be its first passenger with him. I said I felt there were others far more deserving than I to ride it, but, as he pointed out, if I was about to be interviewed on live national television on what the ride was like, I'd better give it a try!

So Keith and I climbed aboard and off we set. I have to admit that I rode it with a considerable degree of trepidation. In order to cram this huge number of inversions into a relatively short length of track there was virtually no space for any adjusting transitions from one configuration to another. Each inversion was literally bolted onto the next. If the engineers had not got their calculations totally right, and the massive steel track bent to absolute perfection, then the ride would be a real "head-banger". We left the station, and immediately dropped into the first barrel roll inversion which was smooth-as-silk. But that was not surprising, as it was the only inversion in the ride that was on its own and not sandwiched between others. We climbed the first lift, and from then on everything became a blur. We tumbled upside down, over and over. In theory I knew every inch of the track, every twist and turn, since I had worked for days on my computer two years previously smoothing out the track and adjusting the inversions. But even I was disoriented. The relentless tumbling and twisting eventually paused as we arrived at the base of the second lift. Although my head was spinning, I was thrilled at how amazingly smooth the ride had been up to that point. But the trickiest section was yet to come. The car tipped us on our backs as the train climbed the vertical lift up to the second and most intense section of the ride. Could this be as smooth and perfect as the first? Again, on leaving the top of the second lift the train had quickly picked up speed and gyrated us through the remainder of the 14 inversions with the same precision and fluidity as in the first half of the circuit. We arrived back in the station two very happy guys. Keith had supervised the construction and I had helped conceive a ride that would undoubtedly knock Nemesis off the number one spot.

But the fact that the ride was a record-breaker in terms of the number of upside-down inversions in the track was irrelevant to me. What was important was that we (that is, a huge team of experienced people) had created THE BEST. A ride that would go on to thrill, entertain and intimidate millions of people. It was time for me to bow out.

As I drove home from Alton Towers for the last time I went through the nearby town of Uttoxeter, and I put on the car radio. Karen Carpenter was singing "We've Only Just Begun" ... the very song that had been playing on that first journey on the way to Barry Island that had started my career in the Theme Park industry. Something told me that one door had closed, but another one was about to open. My career had been more happy and fulfilling than I could ever have dared to imagine. I had met some wonderful people along the way, and, hopefully, given a few million others some fun, thrills and laughter.

So I decided I would embark on one last project of my own. A project that would entertain and amuse.

So I wrote this book.

And I hope you've enjoyed reading it.

Postscript

Since writing the first edition of this book, many nice things have happened. A friend of my old chemistry teacher (remember, the Manfred Mann lookalike?) happened to read the book, and he put me in touch with him. We have exchanged reminiscing correspondence ever since.

And the owner of a circus also read the book, and said he had recently bought a circus clown's car that looked remarkably like the one in the photograph. On further inspection, it turned out to be the vary same! Apparently it had gone through numerous owners, appeared in circuses all around the world, and 43 years later the dear old car is still going strong (even though the doors keep falling off, the radiator explodes, and the backseat collapses ….. but then that's just what it is supposed to do!)

All sorts of lovely people have got in touch with me, and left nice reviews of the book on Amazon, or reminisced about their experiences on my rides when they were children, and how they now take their own children or grandchildren on the same rides. I had the honour of being invited to appear on the BBC Radio 4 "Midweek" programme to talk about it, as well as doing book signings at the theme parks. 2015 was Nemesis's 21st. birthday at Alton Towers, and I was invited back to join in the celebrations.

And in an ironic twist in the tale, in 2018 Alton Towers will be opening a new ride codenamed "SW8". It is a wooden rollercoaster!

Writing "Creating my own Nemesis" has been a most rewarding experience for me.

They say that there is a book in everyone. So what are you waiting for? Get writing! You'll be surprised what a rewarding experience it could be for you too.

JOHN WARDLEY
Cheshire, England
2017

CREATING my own NEMESIS

The autobiography of the man who designed Alton Towers' big rides, and brought the Theme Park to Britain

JOHN WARDLEY

Now available as an audiobook narrated by John Wardley

Obtainable from
Audible, Amazon
iTunes
and other distributors

Made in the USA
San Bernardino, CA
10 November 2018